Satan Has No Authority Over God's Soldier

Satan Has No Authority Over God's Soldier

Illuminating Godlike Faith

R. C. Jette

RESOURCE *Publications* · Eugene, Oregon

SATAN HAS NO AUTHORITY OVER GOD'S SOLDIER
Illuminating Godlike Faith

Copyright © 2019 R. C. Jette. All rights reserved. Except for brief quotations in critical publications or reviews, no part of this book may be reproduced in any manner without prior written permission from the publisher. Write: Permissions, Wipf and Stock Publishers, 199 W. 8th Ave., Suite 3, Eugene, OR 97401.

Resource Publications
An Imprint of Wipf and Stock Publishers
199 W. 8th Ave., Suite 3
Eugene, OR 97401

www.wipfandstock.com

PAPERBACK ISBN: 978-1-5326-9459-2
HARDCOVER ISBN: 978-1-5326-9460-8
EBOOK ISBN: 978-1-5326-9461-5

Manufactured in the U.S.A.　　　　　　　　　JULY 22, 2019

All Scripture references are taken from the King James Version (KJV): KING JAMES VERSION, public domain.

This book is dedicated to all Christians who desire to understand Godlike faith and overcome!

A special thanks is given to my husband, Paul, who has been an inspiration for me to continue doing what the Lord has directed. Also, my daughter, Dawn who has helped me so that I can spend the time writing.

I wish to thank all who have inspired me in some way along my journey of faith!

A heartfelt thanks is given to Wipf and Stock Publishers for their incredible company that has enabled me to become a published author. Their staff have been like family in helping to make the difficulties smooth. I cannot express my gratitude for their previously publishing:

1. *Storms Are Faith's Workout: Preparing Christians for Spiritual Ambush* (2018)
2. *Faith's Journey Confronts Obstacles: Instructing God's Soldiers to Overcome in His Armor* (2019)
3. *Spiritual Shipwreck on the Horizon: Exhorting Christians to Contend for the Faith and Comprehend the Deceitfulness of Sin* (2019)
4. *Satan's Strategy to Torment Through Physical Ambush: Educating God's Soldiers of Satan's Plot to Shatter Faith Through Sickness and Disease* (2019)
5. *The Elfdins and the Gold Temple: An Oralee Chronicle* (2018)
6. *Charlie McGee and the Leprechaun: Life's Curious Twist of Events* (2019)
7. *The Shrines of Manitoba: Dark Secrets Shall Be Brought to Light* (2019)

WHAT AM I

I sit in a place of solitude and assess what I am;
Meditation provokes me to reach into the depths of my heart.
My first evaluation concludes that I am merely human,
But is humanity to accept failure as its lot?

Speculation considers how fragile I often seem to be;
While at other times strength and power rule.
Occasionally, I fight an endless and turbulent sea,
That becomes a slight and tranquil pool.

Oft times, I find my heart engaged in deep thought,
When I'm besieged and believe nothing can be done.
When I hear a whisper that my failures have been bought,
I recall God decreed freedom thru the victory of His Son.

Because of Him, I'm not destined to be trodden down;
His Word declares His will that I'm supposed to rule.
The cross of Calvary replaced my thorns with a crown;
With this truth accepting failure would yield me a fool.

Clarity of thought declares in hardships I'm the boss;
Revelation surges awareness that I'm not decreed a loser.
Conquest is thru faith that God's Son took my loss:
Then tis clear, what I am-I am an overcomer!

— R. C. JETTE

Contents

Introduction | ix

Chapter 1	Godlike Faith Defined	1
Chapter 2	Godlike Faith is a Christian's Essence	6
Chapter 3	Godlike Faith Does Not Worry	10
Chapter 4	Godlike Faith Breaks up the Fallow Ground	15
Chapter 5	Godlike Faith Has a Modus Operandi	21
Chapter 6	Godlike Faith Sleeps During the Storm	27
Chapter 7	Godlike Faith Accepts Suffering	32
Chapter 8	Godlike Faith Builds its Ark	37
Chapter 9	Godlike Faith Discerns God's Voice	45
Chapter 10	Godlike Faith Does Not Fear	53
Chapter 11	Godlike Faith Plants a Good Crop	60
Chapter 12	Godlike Faith is of the Spirit	65
Chapter 13	Godlike Faith Changes the Entailment	72
Chapter 14	Godlike Faith Walks In Authority Over Satan	78

Introduction

ALTHOUGH I have written four previous books concerning faith, I felt impressed to do one that clarifies where faith comes from, what it can do, and how it can be applied to our faith journey. As I have stated before, sometimes seeing things from a different perspective can cause the light of revelation to illuminate what was not understood prior. Too many are not living a victorious life in Christ and need to comprehend what it means to walk by faith.

My previous books were meant to be building blocks for each new book. *Storms Are Faith's Workout* gives an understanding of God's love and how to be victorious when faced with fierce storms of the enemy. *Faith's Journey Confronts Obstacles* was meant to educate God's soldiers in the use of His full armor to prepare us for spiritual warfare. *Satan's Strategy to Torment through Physical Ambush* unfolded a plot by Satan to destroy faith through sickness and disease, and the fallacy that persecution is what wears out the saints of God. *Spiritual Shipwreck on the Horizon* explains why Christians need to contend for the faith and apprehend how the deceitfulness of sin can lead to shipwreck.

God's soldiers seem to forget that we are in the Army of the Lord. Yes, we face a supernatural enemy, but he has no authority over us. He has no power to subdue us, unless we submit to him through sin, unbelief, worry, fear, etc. Christ has subdued Satan and has given us that same authority and power to do likewise.

To those who have read my other books, this will not be a repeat. However, it may touch on some points. I believe that in

INTRODUCTION

order to expand and expound on faith, it is best that I don't replicate the information in my previous books. This one should build on the material in my other books, but not rewrite the others. It will bring forth much added information not hitherto mentioned to help us understand that we can only overcome satanic designs through Godlike faith.

This life is full of storms, obstacles, demonic strategies, etc. In my first book, *Storms Are Faith's Workout*, I stated that I have gained perception through what I have encountered in my spiritual journey to Heaven. I did not acquire this knowledge easily. It came through unremitting persistence, purpose, and perseverance to overcome. If it had come easily, I would not know its worth. I have always held to the truth that the things that are strived for are the things that we cherish the most. I am not referring to salvation. What I am implying is the knowledge, wisdom, and faith that is gained through reading and studying God's Word, and then living that knowledge, wisdom, and faith daily no matter what storm is raging, what obstacle is in our way, or what demonic strategy may be directed at us.

My prayer for you who have picked up this book is that you understand faith, how it works, and the benefits of it. You may have read other books about faith, but you are not yet living an overcoming faith life. Godlike faith is alluding you. Perhaps, you don't truly comprehend what it is all about. Stay with me until the end of the book, and I am sure that your understanding will become enlightened. As your knowledge of what you have in Christ is enhanced, so will be your ability to overcome all storms, obstacles, satanic designs, etc. with Godlike faith!

Chapter 1

Godlike Faith Defined

> Now faith is the substance of things hoped for, the evidence of things not seen (Hebrews 11:1)

According to that scripture, faith is trusting in something that we cannot prove until the evidence is manifested. It is believing without seeing. Our faith is our title deed to what God has promised. As long as we hold fast our faith, we will reap the promise.

It is during the time of the promise (seedtime) and the actuality of the promise (harvest) that many of us can begin to waver. That is the dangerous time for faith. We are not to lean to our own understanding or we will begin to look in the natural for a way to bring about the promise.

Let's expound on the definition of Godlike faith. As we understand what it is, it will revolutionize our faith walk. Too many Christians are not overcoming in life because we don't comprehend the kind of faith that God gave us when we became born again.

> Through faith we understand that the worlds were framed by the word of God, so that things which are seen were not made of things which do appear (Hebrews 11:3).

As I stated in my book, *Faith's Journey Confronts Obstacles*, faith is not of this natural world. It is an attribute of God that is eternal. Faith existed before the creation of the worlds, because it was by His faith that God created all that we now see in the natural.

Unless we understand that there are two worlds co-existing, the spiritual, invisible, and the natural, visible, we will never be enabled to live an overcoming faith life. If we are to effectively serve God, we must keep these two worlds separated. Otherwise, we will find that our faith is like gasoline with water in it. We all know what that means, if we mix water in our gasoline, our car or whatever will spit, sputter, and stop running. That is what is happening to many Christians. Our faith is mixed with something that makes it alloyed and not pure. Therefore, Godlike faith is deficient in our faith walk. Instead of our overcoming the devil, he is taken authority that he does not have. Instead of him being overcome, we are allowing him to overpower us.

Our faith cannot and will not operate, unless we learn to separate the natural world from the supernatural world. Listen to me, that which is carnal, that which is fleshly, and that which is logical will stifle, will smother, will water down our faith.

We cannot mix that which is natural or logical to man with faith. We cannot use carnal or natural principles, precepts, or concepts in the spiritual world. They are powerless and will not be efficacious in developing Godlike faith.

> For though we walk in the flesh, we do not war after the flesh: For the weapons of our warfare are not carnal, but mighty through God to the pulling down of strong holds (2 Corinthians 10: 3-4).

This Scripture is quite obvious that we cannot wage a war of faith with carnal, fleshly, or natural means. Our weapons are not carnal. We can only fight spiritual with spiritual. The devil and his demons can only be conquered through Godlike faith which is a spiritual principle and not a natural principle. We can only fight a supernatural enemy with supernatural authority and power.

> Ye are of God, little children, and have overcome them: because greater is He that is in you, than he that is in the world (1 John 4:4).

In that verse is seen that although Satan is a supernatural power, the power of Christ, the power of God, the indwelling Holy Spirit, or He that is in us, is greater or more powerful than the devil. Jesus made clear that He has given His disciples power or authority over all the power or authority of the devil (Luke 10:19). Satan is defeated and it's time for God's soldiers to walk as the victors and not the vanquished.

Now, we quote Scriptures like that and we claim that there is a natural world and a supernatural world, but do we really understand? I don't believe that we do, or we would be walking in constant victory.

How many times have we said that God created the heaven and the earth? We quote that through Him all things were made and without Him was not anything made that was made (John 1:3). Yet, do we really know what we are saying?

Let's understand more clearly what Godlike faith is. Hebrews 11:3 says that through faith the worlds were framed by the word of God. He spoke it and His faith brought it into existence. Since faith is an attribute of God, He has no unbelief or doubt. As I stated in my previous books, whatever attribute God is, He is totally and completely that attribute. He is one-hundred percent faith. His faith is unalloyed which means that there is not a trace of anything else in it. Unlike us who have faith one minute and the next are full of doubt, God has resolute faith.

Now, Hebrews 11:1 says that faith is the substance of things hoped for, the evidence of things not seen. That is the sum of Godlike faith. Think about that. What did God make all things in this visible world out of? He took that which does not appear to make what we see. In other words, God made all things out of what did not exist before He spoke it into existence through or by His faith. God did not go by what He saw, but by what He believed.

It was by faith that God created all things. God knew His faith could create, make manifest, make visible the heaven and the earth. It was even through His faith that He created the things that are invisible to us in our present state. However, the fact that we do not see them, does not make them any less created. Yet, we believe that God the Father, God the Son, God the Holy Spirit, the angels, devil, demons, etc. exist.

Now, if we can believe in the existence of the spiritual realm that we do not see, why do we waiver in our belief when God gives us a promise in the physical realm? Too many think that it is all about how hard we can believe that will bring forth the manifestation of the promise. And in some cases, we are trying to force God to do what we want and call it faith which is really the sin of presumption.

Let me insert a story about the difference between Godlike faith and presumption that happened many years ago. A couple in the Church were praying for a new home for a family that lived in squalor. The house was full of roaches, food hardened on the kitchen table at least an inch thick, the filth was overpowering, yet, along with the father and mother, there were four teenage children capable of cleaning. Anyway, after we had seen how lazy they were and that they were content to live in that filth, we questioned the couple. They said that if the family could get out of that into a new home that they would change. I told them that God expects us to change where we are and that changing things or changing our location will not change us. When we change, our environment will change. This is seen in our salvation experience. We change inside by the new birth and it begins to transform our outer by what we say, what we do, how we think, how we dress, etc.

They didn't want to hear what I was saying and claimed that their prayer of faith would move God to get a new home for that family. I then suggested that perhaps if they encouraged the teenagers (three were girls) to clean the house that it would make a huge difference in the way they lived. The couple said that it would be easier to teach them to clean in a new house. After several months, they decided that God wanted them to take control. They co-signed for the family to get a new home. In less than a year, the house was just as filthy and full of roaches as their previous home. When the family stopped paying the mortgage, the bank came after the couple for payment.

What I am trying to reveal here is that presuming what God wants or presuming how to help God bring about what you want is not Godlike faith. That couple learned a very hard lesson. We cannot force the hand of God because we believe that our prayer of faith will move Him to do our will and not His. A prayer of faith is not what we will and believing that we can force the hand of God to do our bidding. The prayer of faith is when it is God's will, and we believe Him to bring His will to pass.

What we must understand is that faith does not work in the natural world, in us, or in what we want. Godlike faith is based upon God's will and in His ability to bring forth what He promised. This takes place in the supernatural world where there is no unbelief, doubt, etc.

God believed that nothing was impossible for Him, so He created everything there is in the natural and supernatural realms. Once we comprehend that faith began in God and we understand His ability, we will believe that God can do the impossible. What that means is that faith sees it finished or completed even if the natural eye sees something that is contrary. That is why faith is the substance of things hoped for and the evidence of things not seen.

As we trust God to do His will, Godlike faith is manifested and God makes visible His promise. It is like taking a journey, and we are in the back seat. Faith doesn't keep asking if we are there yet. It sits back and enjoys the scenery along the way and trusts God that He knows what He's doing and how long it will take.

Faith knows that God doesn't need anything that we see in the natural to make something or to do something. Faith believes God's word, even when others may say that it is impossible. Godlike faith is convinced in God's ability to do what He promised and rests in Him until the fulness of His time to bring the promise from the invisible world into the visible world!

Chapter 2

Godlike Faith is a Christian's Essence

> That which is born of the flesh is flesh; and that which is born of the spirit is spirit (John 3:6).

Before we are born again, we do not and cannot possess Godlike faith. We may believe something or say we have faith in this or that. But until we are alive spiritually, we are not capable of faith that supersedes the natural realm. As I stated in my book, *Faith's Journey Confronts Obstacles*, before we are born again, we are spiritually dead. Salvation is a miracle where God transforms us from spiritual death to spiritual life. It is an incredible metamorphosis that enables us to fellowship with the Living God.

That's why Jesus says that unless a man is born again, he cannot see the kingdom of God (John 3:3). When we are born into this world, we are human with human attributes and the human abilities of our parents. We are born of flesh and thereby are flesh. Now, when God performs the miracle and we are born again, we are born of the spirit and thereby are spirit.

Once we are born of the spirit, we have the nature of our Father God. No, we are not God, but we now have His qualities residing in our spirit. Every birth brings forth its kind. Humans bring forth humans. Horses bring forth horses. Birds bring forth birds.

In other words, like begets like. Therefore, it is only reasonable to accept that if we are now born of God, we have His essence like we have the essence of our natural parents.

What are the qualities that we have acquired from our Father God? We now have love, joy, peace, longsuffering, gentleness, goodness, faith, etc. (Galatians 5:22-23). We may have thought we had love, joy, peace, longsuffering, faith, etc. before, but they are limited in ability until we are born again. What I mean by that is that God's love, joy, peace, longsuffering, faith, etc. is perfect. In our flesh, we are not capable of doing anything that is perfect in God's eyes. No matter what we do in our carnal nature, it is nothing but filthy rags. As our faith is alloyed, so is our love, etc. in our flesh. Only as we walk in the spirit can we have Godlike love, joy, faith, etc.

It is obvious as we use our natural qualities of feeding ourselves, dressing ourselves, walking about, speaking to others, etc. that we are human. Now, God gave us certain spiritual qualities so that we can live a supernatural life in this life. What we need to understand is that we show our Godlike essence when we believe God to do what man calls impossible. We exhibit our Godlike essence when we express love instead of anger, hate, etc., when we are verbally attacked by others. We reveal our Godlike essence when we demonstrate a peace that passeth all understanding in the fiercest trials. We display our Godlike essence when we exhibit faith instead of fear, worry, etc.

How many of us are living below the overcoming life? How many of us are living in unbelief because the promise is taking too long? How many of us can't seem to love unless everything is going our way? How many of us do not have the joy of the Lord because of unbelief or doubt? How many of us are struggling day after day because we spend more time in the physical realm and not the spiritual realm?

Let's try to make this more lucid. How many of us would pray for a brain? I mean that sounds ridiculous because we are born with a brain. All the components of humanity are visible when we are born. Yes, due to sin, we have some with physical deformities.

I understand that quite clearly, as Dawn, my oldest daughter, was born with a severe bi-lateral cleft lip and palate. However, there is no sin in the spiritual realm of God, thereby, there is no deformity, lack, or inability in spiritual attributes.

We don't need to pray for a brain. Why are we praying for love, joy, peace, faith, etc., when they are our spiritual attributes through the Holy Spirit after salvation? Too many times our spiritual attributes are not functioning because we are not using them, or we are trying to get something that we already possess. How many times have we prayed for faith? Romans 12:3 makes clear that God has dealt to every man the measure of faith. That means that all His children have been given the measure of faith. He doesn't give a bigger measure to that great Evangelist and a smaller measure to the Sunday School teacher. To believe otherwise would be to accuse God of being a respecter of persons.

The reason that some seem to have greater faith is that we use it. Like I said in my previous book, *Storms Are Faith's Workout*, faith must be exercised in order to become strong. Let me explain it this way. If someone seems to have more love, it is because they have allowed it to become strengthened through forgiveness. The strength of God's love is seen in His forgiving us our sins against Him. It is the same with faith, it's strengthened through use. The more we trust God to get us through the storm, the stronger becomes our faith.

> What? Know ye not that your body is the temple of the Holy Ghost, which is in you, which ye have of God, and ye are not your own? (1 Corinthians 6:19)

According to the above verse, where is the Holy Spirit at present? He is in our body. If He is in us, that means that all His fruit is in us. He is all that God is, for He is God the Spirit. And He is love, joy, peace, kindness, faith, etc. We don't have to wonder if we have God's essence, we know that we do because of the indwelling Holy Spirit. God in us enables us to live a victorious and overcoming life. We have to live in the reality that Satan has no authority or power over us. As we live victoriously, we can effectively be a witness to the world of the existence of God.

When we are born of the flesh, we were equipped with what we needed to live in this world. We think, we see, we hear, we walk, we speak, etc. Yes, the effects of sin may have caused birth defects, but that is because this natural world is defective as a result of sin. However, the consequences of sin have no effects in the supernatural world, for there is no sin or defects in Heaven.

Being born again enabled us to receive the spiritual qualities that are necessary to live a life that takes authority or power over all satanic designs. Whatever our mission, whatever our ministry, whatever our function in the Body of Christ may be, God equipped us to perform in the supernatural as He equipped us to perform in the natural.

If we comprehend that as we were born physically with what we need to live in this life, when we became born again, we were born spiritually with what we need to overcome in this life. As I stated, faith supersedes anything in this realm. It is greater than everything that is part of this natural realm, for it is part of the supernatural realm of God. Since God has equipped us with all we need in the physical, He, likewise, armed us with all we need in the spiritual. As we have human qualities when we are born, Godlike faith is an essence to all who have been born again!

Chapter 3

Godlike Faith Does Not Worry

Therefore I say unto you, Take no thought for your life, what ye shall eat, or what ye shall drink; nor yet for your body, what ye shall put on. Is not the life more than meat, and the body than raiment? Behold the fowls of the air: for they sow not, neither do they reap, nor gather into barns; yet your heavenly Father feedeth them. Are ye not much better than they? Which of you by taking thought can add one cubit unto his stature? And why take ye thought for raiment? Consider the lilies of the field, how they grow; they toil not, neither do they spin: And yet I say unto you, that even Solomon in all his glory was not arrayed like one of these. Wherefore, if God so clothe the grass of the field, which today is, and tomorrow is cast into the oven, shall he not much more clothe you, O ye of little faith? Therefore take no thought, saying, What shall we eat? or, What shall we drink? or, Wherewithal shall we be clothed? (For after all these things do the Gentiles seek:) for your heavenly Father knoweth that ye have need of all these things. But seek ye first the kingdom of God, and his righteousness; and all these things shall be added unto you. Take therefore no thought for the morrow: for the morrow shall take thought for the things of itself. Sufficient unto the day is the evil thereof (Matthew 6:25-34).

T HIS profound passage in Matthew records Jesus' view of worry or anxiety. It is imperative that we truly understand how worry hinders Godlike faith. We are not to worry about life's basic needs, such as food and clothing. Christ makes clear that we have a heavenly Father who knows what we need and He will provide.

When Jesus tells us to take no thought, He is telling us that we are not to be anxious or worry about what we need. It doesn't mean that we are not to go grocery shopping, plan our meals, or think about what we shall eat, drink, or wear. He is wanting us to understand that we are not to worry or to be anxious about such things. If we worry about what God has promised to supply, we are in unbelief. Let's think about that. In the previous chapter, it was revealed that God gave us all we need to live in this life. Why do we doubt that He Who gave us life would refuse to give us that which is necessary to preserve our physical life?

He is mindful of the fowls of the air who do not labor for their food. Yet, He is not their Father. Which of us as parents would allow our child to go without food, clothes, etc.? Although we are not capable of perfect love, we do all that we can to take care of them. How much more would our heavenly Father Who possesses perfect love take care of us? If He willingly gave His Son's life out of love for us, He will meet our physical need of food and clothing.

Yet, we worry about how we are going to get this or that. We worry about how we are going to pay the bills. We worry about how we are going to get that car. We worry about how we are going to afford whatever. Worry seems to dominate us who have Godlike faith residing in us. If we are born again and Spirit filled, we have Godlike faith residing in us through the Holy Spirit. As the fruit of the Spirit grows in us, our Godlike faith gets stronger and stronger.

In the verses in Matthew, the Lord is really claiming that worry is a complete waste of energy and should not be pampered because God provides for our needs. He then appeals to reason about the consequences of worry when He asks, "Which of you by taking thought can add one cubit unto his stature?" Worry and fretting have never manipulated the future and will never do so. Jesus states that the ungodly or unbelievers struggle over having their needs met, but God's soldier trusts God for them.

Christians realize that if we take care of the need of our children, we can be assured that our heavenly Father will do likewise for us. We know that the righteous have never been forsaken, nor our seed begging bread (Psalm 37:25). We know that God shall supply all our need according to his riches in glory by Christ Jesus (Philippians 4:19). We understand that our loving Father will take care of our material, physical, and spiritual needs as we turn them over to Him.

Let me illuminate a factor about worry, anxiety, fretting, etc. They come about when we turn from God, transfer the burdens of our life onto ourselves, and assume that we alone are responsible for handling our life's problems. Instead of acknowledging God's sovereignty and power, or seeking His kingdom and righteousness first, many of us slip into sinful self-reliance and concern with our own life's troubles.

> Come unto me, all ye that labour and are heavy laden, and I will give you rest. Take my yoke upon you, and learn of me; for I am meek and lowly in heart: and ye shall find rest unto your souls (Matthew 11:28-29).

The verses in Matthew reveal what I mean by transferring the burdens of our life onto ourselves. When we worry, we are carrying the load ourselves. We tend to allow the troubles, burdens, hardships, etc. of our life to overwhelm us. Too many of us have not learned that Jesus is the balance beam. I explained about the scale in *Faith's Journey Confronts Obstacles*.

Let me give a brief explanation here. His *yoke* in the Greek means to join; the beam of a balance as connecting the scale. It is the beam that joins the pans on either side of the scale. One pan has the weights and the other pan has the load or that which is being weighed. Without the weights in the opposite pan, the load would drop. It is like a seesaw. If one gets off, the other stays on the ground.

The heavy burdens of this life that could drain our strength and cause us to collapse under the load is balanced when we come to Jesus and take His yoke upon us. We have to quit trying to carry things in our strength, in our knowledge, in our wisdom, in our education, etc. Verse 29 says, *Take my yoke upon you, and learn of me.* Jesus will teach us how He balances the heavy load. Without Jesus, there is no beam to balance our load, and we are carrying it all. Each day, we can sometimes find that our load gets heavier with new burdens. Only as we yoke up with Christ is the load balanced and we find rest for our soul. In Faith's Journey, I explained this in more detail. However, for this book, it is imperative that we understand that without Godlike faith, we will not trust Jesus and will continue to carry the burdens ourselves.

When we dwell on our problems, we become worried and frustrated. These emotions are destructive to faith. They reveal a lack of trust in God and a doubt that He loves us. We forget that He is in control. Godlike faith does not worry or become frustrated. We need to trust in the Lord to meet our need, give ourselves to Him for His use and safekeeping, and we will find peace. Instead of the destructive emotions, we will have constructive emotions that will build our faith.

According to Matthew 6:25-34, there are seven reasons that we should not worry.

1. The same God Who created life in us can be trusted with the details of our life.
2. Worrying about the future impedes our efforts for today.
3. Worrying is destructive to faith.
4. God does not ignore those who depend upon Him.
5. Worry shows a lack of faith and understanding of God.
6. There are real challenges God wants us to pursue, and worrying keeps us from them.
7. Living one day at a time keeps us from being consumed with worry about tomorrow.

Let me ask a question. Do we know how many hairs that we have on our head? God knows every hair of our head (Matthew 10:30). If we have no control of their number, why do we think that we can control other aspects of our life? God is the controller. He alone knows the beginning from the end. He alone knows what we need and what we do not need. If we would spend the energy that we waste with worrying on seeking the things of God's kingdom, we would be surprised how soon all those gigantic troubles would seem as trivial nothings. We have no need that God is not aware of. We have no need that God is not able to meet. Thus, in reality, we have no need to worry!

Chapter 4

Godlike Faith Breaks up the Fallow Ground

> Sow to yourselves in righteousness, reap in mercy, break up your fallow ground: for it is time to seek the Lord, till he come and rain righteousness upon you (Hosea 10:12).

FALLOW ground refers to land that has become hardened and cannot receive seed. This is implying that the hardened heart cannot receive God's word to grow thereby. We cannot possess Godlike faith without a heart that can be molded in the Potter's hand (Isaiah 64:8). Only a heart of flesh can receive the seed of His word and be transformed from a broken vessel into a mended vessel useful to the Potter. God takes all our brokenness and makes us mended.

Many in the Church are seeking for more faith. Yet, only a small number are walking in faith or by faith. It troubled me as this reality became more apparent. When I sought the Lord, He said that it is because there is not a proper understanding in the Church as to what faith really is. There are all kinds of books, teachings, tapes, etc. on faith. However, as good as some of these sound, there is too much of man's interpretation and too little of God's illumination.

We have to understand that Godlike faith is not accomplished in ten easy steps to great faith or faith for dummies, etc. As

I have stated in my other books, a body builder is not born with big muscles. Muscles don't build up by sitting around and taking it easy. They are built by strenuous and continuous exercise. I made this clear in *Storms Are Faith's Workout*. The difference between building fleshly muscles and spiritual muscles that strengthen our faith is that one is by physical means and the other is by spiritual means.

Godlike faith is built by continuously exercising spiritual principles. The weights that we use are tests, trials, hardships, storms, obstacles, etc. However, if we do not break up the fallow ground, we will not be enabled to allow the seed of God's word to grow and strengthen our faith.

> For my thoughts are not your thoughts, neither are your ways my ways, saith the Lord (Isaiah 55:8).

What God calls faith is not what man calls faith. God wants strong soldiers of faith in His army. He wants us to comprehend what He expects from us concerning faith. What too many in the Church are calling faith is not really faith at all. According to Hosea 4:6, God's people are destroyed for lack of knowledge.

Because many of us are believing or listening to different teachings, we are being destroyed because we lack knowledge of the Scriptures. I mean comprehension of sound doctrine or that which rightly divides the word of truth. This lack has many young or immature Christians beguiled by man's philosophy of faith and are confused. Some are leaving the faith when things don't turn out like we wanted or expected.

Why are we leaving? It is because the teachings that we are reading, hearing, etc. are not sound. I mean in accordance to the whole counsel of God's word. As we keep listening to the wrong doctrine, we are becoming hardened to truth. Whereas, if we would break up the fallow ground and receive the truth of God's word by studying the Scriptures, we would recognize the error in the teachings that we are accepting.

> But the anointing which ye have received of him abideth in you, and ye need not that any man teach you: but as

the same anointing teacheth you of all things, and is truth, and is no lie, and even as it hath taught you, ye shall abide in him (1 John 2:27).

The anointing is the Holy Spirit that resides in us who are born again. He will lead us into all truth (John 16:13). The Apostle John is saying that the Holy Spirit will teach us to recognize the spirit of antichrist or false teaching. As we read and study our Bible, we are putting truth into our spirit. Then when there is a false teaching or false doctrine, the Holy Spirit of truth will quicken us. The teaching will not bear witness with our spirit. Even if we are young in the Lord and at first don't understand what is wrong, our spirit will be quickened that something is wrong.

Let me interject a story here that happened when I was a young Christian. My husband and I were listening to this preacher while getting ready for Church. Anyway, I sensed a quickening in my spirit that what he was saying was wrong. Immediately, I told my husband who was younger in the Lord than me that the Holy Ghost was impressing me that something is wrong. He shut it off. Anyway, after we prayed, it was apparent that he was a false teacher, for the Holy Spirit quickened me to 1 Peter 1:16. The preacher claimed that God doesn't expect us to be holy to get to Heaven, He just expects us to live a life that does good works. He used the Scripture from James about faith without works is dead. Yet, Peter makes clear that we are to be holy as God is holy.

However, I couldn't have been quickened without the word of God in me. The truth of God's word revealed the erroneous teaching. It is imperative in these last days where self-lovers, lovers of pleasures, hirelings, etc. will be prevalent that we discern the true and false teachers. However, we cannot discern without a knowledge of the Scriptures. In order for the word to get into us, we must break up the fallow ground. That means that we need to dig up any preconceived notions of ours. We have to be teachable and recognize that we don't know everything. It is admitting that we may have believed erroneous teachings. Stubbornness of spirit has kept many of God's soldiers from growing and receiving strong meat that will help us to discern both good and evil.

As a builder constructs a house, the ground must be prepared before the footings of the foundation can be put in. Once the foundation is finished, the rest of the house is constructed. But if the foundation is unstable, the whole building will be volatile. Without a firm foundation, we have no stable ground to stand upon. This truth was revealed more fully in my book about Storms.

Scriptures make plain that God is not a respecter of persons (Romans 2:11). Yet, some of us are moving mightily in Godlike faith while others of us are not. The reason is not that some Christians have faith and some don't. It is due to the fact that many of us do not know what faith really is. Now, let's not get flummoxed because we don't have all the answers in this chapter. It is building upon each chapter that will help us to finally understand what Godlike faith is.

God wants to answer every prayer that we pray. However, if just praying would bring results, we would already have the world saved. It's not just prayer that is needful, but knowing how to pray in faith. What we must comprehend is that the Lord wants Godlike faith working in our lives. We are supposed to represent Jesus by walking in victory every day. According to Mark 16:17-18, healings, signs, miracles are supposed to be following us.

Before the fallow ground can be broken up, before Godlike faith can even be operative in our lives, there is a first step. Without spiritual birth, we cannot have Godlike faith. We cannot see or perceive spiritual principles (John 3:3). Unless we are born again, we cannot see or understand the things of God.

It has nothing to do with seeing Heaven; that is the afterlife. For all believers that follow Jesus are promised eternal life. This seeing means spiritual eyesight to see what the natural or the unregenerate man cannot see.

Some have asked me how we can know that we are born again. It is quite simple, when we encounter the living God through Jesus Christ, our life changes. As I revealed in Faith's Journey, it is a total metamorphosis like the caterpillar to butterfly. Our desires, likes, etc. change from fleshly to that which pleases God. If our life has not had a drastic change, then we had a head salvation and not a heart changing experience. I know this truth, because it happened to me. That is told in the same book about Faith's Journey.

> That which is born of the flesh is flesh; and that which is born of the Spirit is spirit (John 3:6).

We must be born again, born of the Spirit of God to see, to perceive, to understand spiritual principles. Godlike faith is one of these spiritual principles or things that cannot be seen or perceived until we are born again. That which is flesh is flesh and that which is spirit is spirit. We are either walking in the flesh or in the spirit. This truth was revealed in my book, *Spiritual Shipwreck on the Horizon* in chapter four.

Do we want our prayers answered, do we want the sick healed, do we want to live the abundant life in Christ? If we do, the first step is to be born again. Most of us are reading this and thinking that I am born again. However, I am not living a victorious Godlike faith life. This book should reveal the answers to us as we read to the end. This chapter is meant to teach us that we must break up the fallow ground. We must get rid of our stubbornness, our wanting things our way, our contentment with the teachers of itching ears, our desiring our flesh to be pampered, etc.

Before we are saved, faith can never be operative in our life. I mean Godlike faith, genuine faith. We can claim to have faith, but it is only a figure of speech. A spiritual principle cannot be operative or working in a natural or physical person, because faith is a supernatural principle. How do I know that? God's word reveals that faith is an essence of God. It was by His faith that God created all things (Hebrews 11:3). God is Spirit and His essence is given to us through the indwelling Holy Spirit.

If we are to break up the fallow ground, we must repent of sin in our life. Repentance will soften our minds and hearts to the truth of God's word. As we do that, the Holy Spirit plants His fruit in us that enables our life to conform to His will and not ours. Faith is not a natural principle; it is a supernatural principle. It only works in the spiritual realm and not in the physical realm. Therefore if we are in the flesh, there is no Godlike faith. Only as we are in the spirit do we manifest Godlike faith. That's why He must increase and we must decrease (John 3:30). The more of Him and the less of us means that we are breaking up the fallow ground and allowing Godlike faith to grow in us!

Chapter 5

Godlike Faith Has a Modus Operandi

> But the hour cometh, and now is, when the true worshippers shall worship the Father in spirit and in truth: for the Father seeketh such to worship him. God is a Spirit: and they that worship him must worship him in spirit and in truth (John 4:23-24).

THIS chapter is challenging because it is concerned with the lack of Godlike faith in the lives of many naming the Name of Jesus as Savior. It is imperative that we comprehend the cause for so little manifestations of faith in the lives of Christians. Without understanding that true worshippers worship in Spirit and truth, we will not manifest Godlike faith in our life.

Godlike faith cannot work in the selfishness that seems to be controlling much of Christianity. Faith cannot and will not work or be effective in the lives of us who insist on walking in our flesh and obeying its lusts.

If we would remember that faith is a spiritual principle, we can begin to recognize why faith is not working. Perhaps, we are in the flesh where spiritual principles cannot function. Only as we separate the spiritual (supernatural) realm from the natural (physical) realm will we start to realize how Godlike faith is possible.

Faith is spiritual in origin. It is not of the natural realm and cannot work or be effective in our flesh. It is an attribute of God. Because of the indwelling Holy Spirit, Who is God in us, faith is also an attribute of us who are born again.

> Now the works of the flesh are manifest, which are these; Adultery, fornication, uncleanness, lasciviousness, idolatry, witchcraft, hatred, variance, emulations, wrath, strife, seditions, heresies, envyings, murders, drunkenness, revellings, and such like: of the which I tell you before, as I have also told you in time past, that they which do such things shall not inherit the kingdom of God (Galatians 5:19-21).

> But the fruit of the Spirit is love, joy, peace, longsuffering, gentleness, goodness, faith, meekness, temperance: against such there is no law. And they that are Christ's have crucified the flesh with the affections and lusts (Galatians 5:22-24).

Do we see faith listed in the works of the flesh? As we read the pursuits of our flesh, we cannot find faith itemized. Now, let's read the fruit of the Spirit. As we read the fruit, we find faith listed. The reason we do not find faith in the works of the flesh is because it is spiritual in essence. It is not possible in the flesh.

As a matter of fact, all the components of the fruit of the Spirit are spiritual. We cannot enjoy any of the fruit when walking in the flesh. Let me show further this truth. Can we find peace in the works of the flesh? Is there any self-control? Is there any love? Of course not, because all the works are based on selfishness. It is all that natural man indulges himself in. There is no denying self in the flesh.

It takes self-denial to walk in the Spirit. We can only love the unlovely in the Spirit. It is not easy to have self-control or temperance when someone is screaming profanities at us or trying to pick a fight with us.

> And he said to them all, if any man will come after me, let him deny himself, and take up his cross daily, and follow me (Luke 9:23).

We wonder why Godlike faith is not operative in us. If we would take a closer look at our life, we would find that much of it is producing the works of the flesh. How many times are we reacting in anger? How many times do we feel envy or jealousy? How many times do we have sinful desires? How many times do we worship self by indulging in the lusts of the flesh, the lusts of the eyes, and the pride of life? Then we question why faith is not operating in our life. How can faith be operative in a life that spends most of the time walking in the works of the flesh?

> Neither yield ye your members as instruments of unrighteousness unto sin: but yield yourselves unto God, as those that are alive from the dead, and your members as instruments of righteousness unto God. For sin shall not have dominion over you: for ye are not under the law, but under grace (Romans 6:13-14).

John 8:36 states that Jesus has made us free. What is it that we have been freed from? John 8:34 makes clear that it is sin. When Jesus rose from the dead, He took all power from the devil. Satan no longer has power over us. The world says, "The devil made me do it." Well, that may be true since the devil can take over those that are not saved at his will (2 Timothy 2:26). Howbeit, he cannot take over a child of God. This is backed up in the Scriptures. No where does a demon possess a child of God. All that Jesus delivered from demonic spirits were unbelievers.

The verses in Romans make clear that we are the ones in control of our body. It tells us to not yield our members as instruments of unrighteousness. In other words, we are not to allow our body to sin. Only we have the dominion over our self. That power belongs to us and not the devil. It is crucial that God's soldiers realize that Satan has no power or authority over us.

When we give way to sin, we cannot blame anyone else. Too many blame our husband, our wife, our mother, our father, our sister, our brother, our children, our uncle, our aunt, our boss, etc. It's always someone else that is to blame when we yield to our flesh.

I want to reveal this more clearly. We need to understand that our body is a vineyard that is capable of growing either the fruit of the Spirit or the works of the flesh. If one is watered and cultivated and one is not, which one grows? Of course, the tree that is watered and cultivated will flourish.

Now, I want us to see a tree claiming to be a Christian. It is thriving with the works of the flesh. Then, let's picture that same tree where the fruit is withering and dying. Do we appear to be a Christian? No, we do not. When the works of the flesh flourish, we look, act, talk, etc. like an unbeliever. We must understand that no spiritual principle is at work in us when we walk in the flesh. When we exercise the works of the flesh there is no visible fruit in our life.

Let's look at a tree claiming to be a Christian that has presented or yielded our body to the Spirit. We are flourishing in the fruit of the Spirit. Okay, now look at that same tree where the works of flesh is withering and dying. Do we appear to be a Christian? Yes, of course we do. When the fruit of the Spirit is flourishing, we look, act, talk, etc. like Jesus. If we are reviled, we keep our flesh under. What this means is that we are exercising the fruit of the Spirit and there is no visible works of the flesh in our life.

Some of us are probably wondering what all this has to do with faith's modus operandi. It has much to do with it, because faith has a procedure that must be followed to bring forth positive results. This involves faith's answer time and the fact manifestation time. Because the principle involves two worlds, we must separate them for faith to be effective.

Faith's answer time concerns the spirit or the invisible world. The fact manifestation time concerns the natural or visible world.

> Therefore I say unto you, what things soever ye desire, when ye pray, believe that ye receive them, and ye shall have them (Mark 11:24).

According to the verse in Mark, when is faith's answer time? If we believe that we have received them, it is when we pray. Now, if the faith's answer time concerns the spirit world, where is the answer to our prayer? It is in Heaven. Let me explain this more clearly. The Lord has impressed you not to give up on your husband but to pray for his salvation. You are praying for your husband's salvation and he's at the bar flirting with the women.

Remember, faith is a spiritual truth, so you believe he is saved by faith in the spirit world, in the mind of God. The moment you pray the prayer of faith, it is done in Heaven. God sees him saved, Spirit filled, and hands raised praising God. This is faith's answer time. It happens the moment the prayer of faith is uttered.

Okay, your husband comes home from the bar, cursing, and downright belligerent. What are you going to do? Faith says he's saved. Fact says he's acting like the devil. This is where we have to choose to believe faith or fact. It is our choice. If we give into our flesh, we tie the hands of God.

> But without faith it is impossible to please him: for he that cometh to God must believe that he is, and that he is a rewarder of them that diligently seek him (Hebrews 11:6).

When we come to God in prayer according to His will, He expects us to believe that He is and believe that we have our answer. Pay attention, faith is a spiritual truth, so we receive our answer by faith.

When it was believed for that husband's salvation, by faith he was saved. But down here, he isn't. Since faith is the greater truth, the superseding truth, God then begins to go to work in the circumstances and situations. It may take a day, a week, a month, a year, or years. But as long as we continue in the faith, lined up with the word, God will bring about the fact manifestation in the visible realm.

God wants to answer or bring forth faith's answer time to fact manifestation time. He desires to bless us. It is imperative that we comprehend that we must get our answers by faith before we get them by fact. Our answered prayers are invisible before they are visible (Hebrews 11:1). They are answered in the spirit world before we see them in the natural world. When we have believed by faith, we must then hold fast to God's word. In His time, He will make it a fact.

Let me reiterate some truths of this chapter:

1. Faith cannot work in the flesh.
2. Faith is an attribute of God.
3. God is not flesh; He is Spirit.
4. Since faith is a spiritual attribute, it can only work when we are in the Spirit.
5. God created all things according to Hebrews 11:3 by His faith.
6. Although our prayers are answered immediately in Heaven, they are only fact manifested by our faith in God's time.

Godlike faith has a modus operandi that God adheres to. We pray, believe He has answered, then live in that belief until fact manifestation takes place. This truth was revealed in my book, *Storms Are Faith's Workout*. In it, I showed that between seedtime (the time of the promise) there is the storm time (the trial of our faith). There is no harvest (fact manifestation) before the storms.

It is during the time of faith's answer and fact manifestation that it is imperative that we have learned the importance of worshipping God in Spirit and truth. If we yield to our flesh that is tired of waiting, we will either give up or try to take things into our own hands.

Whenever we believe God for that answered prayer or a promise, we must learn to expect storms, trials, obstacles, etc. They are not to shipwreck us, but to strengthen our faith. Godlike faith has a modus operandi, God has established how faith works. We must adhere to His plan. First, we believe that as soon as the prayer of faith was uttered, it was answered. Second, we must expect to undergo storms or trials before we see it in the natural realm. Third, when the fullness of God's time has come, we will receive the fact manifestation. Faith is the substance of things hoped for; the evidence of things not seen. That means that our answer is invisible, but Godlike faith sees its fact manifestation!

Chapter 6

Godlike Faith Sleeps During the Storm

> And the same day, when the even was come, he saith unto them, Let us pass over unto the other side. And when they had sent away the multitudes, they took him even as he was in the ship. And there were also with him other little ships. And there arose a great storm of wind, and the waves beat into the ship, so that it was now full. And he was in the hinder part of the ship, asleep on a pillow: and they awake him, and say unto him, Master, carest thou not that we perish? And he arose, and rebuked the wind, and said unto the sea, Peace, be still. And the wind ceased, and there was a great calm. And he said unto them. Why are ye so fearful? how is it that ye have no faith? And they feared exceedingly, and said one to another, What manner of man is this, that even the wind and the sea obey him? (Mark 4:35-41).

ALTHOUGH these verses were the nucleus for my first book, I don't believe that we can ever glean all its nuggets. Sometimes a little twist in familiar passages of Scripture can bring forth a deeper revelation.

It's obvious that it was nighttime when Jesus commanded that He and the disciples pass over the sea from Galilee to the region of the Gadarenes. He had spent a long day teaching and as a man, Jesus experienced the human weakness of fatigue and fell asleep.

Before I continue, I want to expound an important fact that cannot be over emphasized. Too many times, Christians tend to see Jesus as God and not a man. While Jesus was on this earth, He was a man.

> Who, being in the form of God, thought it not robbery to be equal with God: But made himself of no reputation, and took upon him the form of a servant, and was made in the likeness of men: And being found in fashion as a man, he humbled himself, and became obedient unto death, even the death of the cross (Philippians 2:6-8).

This Scripture means that Christ emptied Himself not of His divine nature, but the use of His divine attributes. In other words, He emptied Himself of His ability to do miracles as God. All that Jesus did while here was through the power of the Holy Spirit. The understanding of this fact is vital to our walking in Godlike faith. We cannot ever achieve such faith unless we know that Jesus did all that He did on earth as a man yielded to the Holy Spirit.

Okay, we know what happened after Jesus fell asleep. A sudden storm arose. Apparently, when they started, the sea was calm. It seems that the Sea of Galilee is geographically situated in a basin between two mountains that makes it susceptible to sudden storms. So, that accounts for the sudden storm. However, it also helps us to understand spiritually that we can begin in a calm sea and suddenly be in vicious storm.

The main concern of this chapter is our reaction during the storm. As we look at the disciples, they accuse Jesus of not caring. Why was He asleep when they were about to be destroyed or killed. Of course, Jesus gets up and says, "Peace be still." He commanded the storm to be dumb or to be silent. Then, He turns and reprimands the disciples for their unbelief.

Now, let's get to the crux or meat of this chapter. As we visualize the situation, we see a storm so violent that the boat's rocking back and forth, roaring winds, and the waves are pouring water in the boat. We see the disciples frantic; they are in a frenzy of fear and worry. Yet, we see Jesus in the back of the boat, asleep, and in perfect peace.

This is so important to understand. Before us are two camps. The one is Faith's calm or Godlike faith and the other is unbelief's storm or unbelief. The definition of faith is complete trust, complete confidence, or steadfast belief. The definition of unbelief is lack of belief which means a lack of trust, a lack of confidence, or a pliable belief.

Unbelief is pliable, changes to whatever wind blows. It is fickle, unstable, changeable, etc. It sees only what it experiences. It feels the boat rocking, sees the waves filling the boat with water, and believes the sea is threatening them with death. We must understand that unbelief sees only what it's feeling, what it's enduring, what it's encountering, and what it views in the natural realm at present. All it sees is its fears, its worries, its pain, its finances, whatever. Unbelief sees the storm and its threats.

Godlike faith is firm and cannot be moved, never gives up, and never surrenders. This kind of faith doesn't see the encounter. It sees the promise of God. Instead of looking at the boat full of water or the raging storm, faith sees the power and grace of God.

The great characteristic and power of Godlike faith is to see what is not visible (Hebrews 11:1). Faith doesn't look at what it sees in the natural realm, because faith knows it's a lie. Why is the natural usually a lie? Because what we see is contrary to the promise of God. Like the woman promised the salvation of her husband, Godlike faith doesn't pay attention to the natural. It looks beyond to the promise in the supernatural. Faith doesn't think that with God nothing shall be impossible (Luke 1:37). Godlike faith knows that with God nothing shall be impossible.

Some of us are thinking that all this is fine, but what does it have to do with our Scripture text. It has everything to do with it. Let me show what I mean. We see that Jesus said, "Let us pass over unto the other side." This is a command, a commission, or a promise. He didn't say that we need to try to pass over to the other side. He was positive that we are to pass over.

Jesus did always the will of the Father Who sent Him and it was God's will for them to go over to the other side. If it was God's will, then Jesus knew that He and the disciples would get to the other side. God cannot lie (Numbers 23:19, Titus 1:2). When God promises something, He is going to complete it.

This is a vital point that we must comprehend. If and when God tells us to do something or has promised us something, know for a fact that a sudden storm will come. It may take any form of opposition, discouragement, etc. It may feel as though all Hell has come up against us. In a way it has, for Satan never wants us to do God's will or receive what God promises.

Please understand that we will not receive a command or a promise from the Lord without encountering a storm after the word. Jesus knew this, but He was in perfect peace. Was it because He was God? No, because He was totally yielded to the Holy Spirit. It was through faith in God that He could sleep during the storm. Think about that. What did He have to fear? He trusted God to complete what He told Him to do. He knew that He would not die before it was God's time. We need to stop allowing the devil's lying storms to put fear in us.

At this time, I want to interject a story that happened to me many years ago. There was this situation and I was overwhelmed. As I was praying, I had a vision of being in the middle of an ocean and I couldn't see land. I went to stand up and couldn't find the bottom. When I came back up, I cried, "Lord help me! I can't swim. I can't see any land." As I'm frantic in the water trying to stay up, the Lord said, "Be still, take deep breaths, be calm. Now, lay back, let the water hold you. Close your eyes, rest, and the current will take you into land."

As I did that, Scripture promises flooded my mind (Philippians 4:6-7; Isaiah 26:3; 1 John 4:18; John 4:18). Then I went from the vision to me in prayer and I jumped up and said, "Lord, I get it. I understand that Godlike faith sleeps during the storm and has perfect peace, because it trusts God. Faith doesn't dwell on the storm; it looks beyond to God Who is able to calm the storm. It is taking our natural eyes off the storm and looking with our spiritual eyes to God.

Now, like I said, we will not receive a command or a promise from God without a storm, trial, etc. I have made this evident in my other books. This book is meant to unfold what Godlike faith is. We must remember Who God is and that He can do anything. We need to look beyond the storm, the trial, the obstacle, etc. and see His promise, His ability, and that the word of His power upholds all things (Hebrews 1:3).

Some of us may have been eyeing the storm and have been caught up in its winds, rain, etc. Others of us may have been endlessly trying to rid the boat of water and have become weary. Some of us may have been overwhelmed by the ferocity of the storm and find ourselves doubting or wavering in our belief in the promise. Some of us may have been accusing God of not caring. Others of us may be convinced that we will drown because we can't swim.

Jesus said, "Let us go," which implies His promise to us. Did we expect a promise without a storm, without a trial, or without a test of our faith? Our problem is that we can become like the disciples during the storm. However, God knows His promise to us to get us to the other side of the storm. He sees the storm, but He doesn't doubt His ability to perform what He said. Jesus is our example of Godlike faith; He was a storm sleeper.

The Lord has been with us in the storm, trial, sickness, disease, etc. God has not forgotten His promise. He always rewards Godlike faith. Know and believe that to some of us, He is about to speak "Peace be still" to that storm!

Chapter 7

Godlike Faith Accepts Suffering

> For unto you it is given in the behalf of Christ, not only to believe on him, but also to suffer for his sake (Philippians 1:29).

SUFFERING and service go hand in hand for the Christian. If we believe that once we are saved that we have a life of tiptoeing through the tulips, we will never cultivate Godlike faith. That's why many fell by the wayside from the prosperity preachers that promised that if we come to Christ, we will never have another concern.

This chapter is meant to illuminate that we cannot be in the Lord's service without partaking of His suffering. Our faith is not strengthened on the mountain top. It is in the valley of trials, storms, hardships, etc. that Godlike faith is cultivated and strengthened.

> Wherein ye greatly rejoice, though now for a season, if need be, ye are in heaviness through manifold temptations: That the trial of your faith, being much more precious than of gold that perisheth, though it be tried with fire, might be found unto praise and honour and glory at the appearing of Jesus Christ (1 Peter 1:6-7).

It is imperative as we go through the trials or sufferings of this life that we do not become discouraged because of their difficulties. As we remain faithful to Christ during the times where the purifying fire is turned up, we will be refined as pure gold. Having our faith purified will result in Godlike faith that will enable us to endure whatever we may have to go through. The encouraging part of the refiner's fire is that our faith is far more valuable than pure gold. When we come through, our life gives praise, honor, and glory to God.

> Beloved, think it not strange concerning the fiery trial which is to try you, as though some strange thing happened unto you: But rejoice, inasmuch as ye are partakers of Christ's sufferings; that, when his glory shall be revealed, ye may be glad also with exceeding joy (1 Peter 4:12-13).

As Christians, we should expect fiery trials. Scripture makes obvious that storms, obstacles, demonic strategies, etc. are inevitable for followers of Christ. Yet, so many of us react as if something foreign is happening when we are faced with troubles, difficulties, suffering, etc.

The sharing in His sufferings is the only way to develop Godlike faith that overcomes the fiery trials that try to destroy us. When Christ returns, we will be overjoyed because as we partook of His sufferings here, we will partake of His glory there.

To be God's child means that this life at times will bring hurt and suffering. However, if we have learned to trust Him, we will in the difficulties turn directly and immediately to Him. In fact, if we are living for Him, problems in our life are usually a sign that we are devoted to Christ.

It is through the sufferings that we go through that enables God to form within us the quality of character that will mold us more into the image of Jesus. If we endure the increase of suffering, we will become strengthened in our resolve to fight sin, the devil, etc. It is time to learn that sufferings are normal, but that Satan doesn't have authority over us. We have power over all that comes our way to be victorious over them and through them.

> So went Satan forth from the presence of the Lord, and smote Job with sore boils from the sole of his foot unto his crown, And he took him a potsherd to scrape himself withal; and he sat down among the ashes (Job 2:7-8).

The book of Job reveals that suffering is a sign of devotion to God and proves that fidelity to Him does not equate exemption from suffering. Christians really need to receive the revelation that without the things that we suffer, we will never develop Godlike faith that overcomes in this life. In my other books, I made evident that storms, obstacles, demonic strategies, etc. are necessary to strengthen our faith.

In the day of prosperity it may be occasionally difficult to say whether we are a Christian or not. However, if when in the time of trouble, we make straight for Christ, we know for certain whose we are and who we serve.

Listen to me, suffering, affliction, trials, etc. are the lot of Christians and non-Christians. We all grieve, face sorrow associated with significant loss. Whether it is death, divorce, loss of a job, loss of a home, etc. In all there is grief. Suffering causes grief to all of us.

> Jesus said unto her, I am the resurrection, and the life: he that believeth in me, though he were dead, yet shall he live: and whosoever liveth and believeth in me shall never die. Believest thou this? (John 11:25-26)

Christians have a foundation that makes our grieving different from the grieving of those without Christ. The knowledge that Christ rose from the dead, prepares the way for acceptance of the fact that we will be resurrected when the Lord returns. This realization enables us to have hope in the face of any sorrow.

As God's soldiers, we believe that we shall rise again, not disembodied, but clothed in a bodily form. But do we realize that we shall rise again with our own body, in our very flesh. The only difference is that we will be healed and immortal. Our body shall be deathless and glorious as the body of Jesus when He arose from the dead.

Jesus says that He is the resurrection and the life, he that believeth in Me, though he were dead, yet shall he live. And whosoever liveth and believeth in me shall never die. Believest thou this?

Do we understand what Jesus is promising or saying here? He is telling us that this life and the life to come are not two lives, but one and the same. Death is not the ending of one and the resurrection the beginning of another. Through all, there runs one imperishable life.

Let me explain. A river which plunges into the earth is buried for a while, then it bursts forth more mightily, and in a fuller tide. It is not two rivers, but one continuous stream. It is the same river that was buried in the earth only to come forth mightier.

The light of today is not quenched at sunset and rekindled at sunrise tomorrow. It is one broad and luminous sun. Today's sun is the same sun that will appear tomorrow. So it is with life and death. Our soul is immortal, an image of God's own eternity.

Few of us realize that as we die, so shall we rise. As there is not a new beginning of our life, so there is no new beginning of our character. The stream which buries itself cloudy and turbid shall rise clouded and foul. The waters that pass clear and bright into the earth shall rise from it clear and bright again.

Consecration is lacking in most Christians. We are not wholly devoted to God and His kingdom. Think about this. It took one day to deliver Israel out of Egypt, but it took forty years to get Egypt out of Israel.

Hear me, we must get the world and its pleasures out of us. Our character determines how we will be resurrected. Our character is our will and what we will is who we are. Character is the total quality of our behavior, as revealed in our habits of thought and expression, our attitudes, our interests, our actions, our personal philosophy of life. It is what we are. Thus, what we will is who we are.

Our will contains our whole intention and sums up our spiritual nature. Our soul bent on rebellion here will break forth then into the full measure of its spiritual wickedness. In other words, it dies wicked and will resurrect in full wickedness.

Our soul bent on consecrating itself wholly to God and has been striving to be holy will be made holy. What this is saying is that whatever we are here, we will be the fullness of it in the resurrection. If we are without Christ, we will spend eternity in Hell without Him. If we have Christ, we will spend eternity in Heaven with Him.

What is all this revealing? If we don't go through the sufferings, we will not cultivate Godlike character and Godlike faith. Without such here, there will be no such quality in the resurrection. It is clear that without suffering, we cannot be perfected.

We must realize that whatever we are here is what we will be in the resurrection. All of us will be resurrected either to the resurrection of life or the resurrection of death. However, those being resurrected in the resurrection of life will be perfect. We will have no flaws or deformities that have been caused by the sin in this world. It will be a perfect body.

Most important is our character. Whatever our character is here is what it will be there. If it is not striving to be holy, righteous, and godly like Christ, it will not be such in the hereafter. Once we comprehend that all of us will be resurrected either to eternal life or to eternal damnation, it causes us to reevaluate our life and desire to change whatever is not pleasing to God.

It is time for us who claim to be Christians to consider wholeheartedly which resurrection we are conforming our character to. Christ's learned obedience by the things He suffered (Hebrews 5:8). How much more should we accept sufferings to conform our character into that of Christs? Godlike faith accepts suffering to cultivate Christlike character!

Chapter 8

Godlike Faith Builds its Ark

> By faith Noah, being warned of God of things not seen as yet, moved with fear, prepared an ark to the saving of his house; by the which he condemned the world, and became heir of the righteousness which is by faith (Hebrews 11:7)

THIS chapter will expound on Godlike faith in a manner that will enlighten our understanding of what faith in God does. We have all read the story of Noah in Genesis and are aware of his building the ark and the wickedness of man at that time.

Genesis 6:9 states that Noah was a just man and perfect in his generation. I want us to contemplate that statement while remembering that Genesis 6:5 states that the wickedness of man was great in the earth, and that every imagination of the thoughts of his heart was only evil continually.

Noah lived in a day where depravity was the characteristic of most of mankind except for the eight that entered into the ark. The wickedness of man's heart was so evil that God had to destroy all living in order to maintain a Godly line. At times, we can feel that's what it is like now. However, if we look closely, we find that God still has His faithful followers as He told Elijah (1 Kings 19:18).

Anyway, let's consider Noah. He was a Godly man that when warned by God of things not seen, moved with fear, prepared an ark to the saving of his house. Amidst the self-loving, corruption, and grief to God, stood a man who believed God. He did not yield to his own understanding.

I want us to think about that. Noah did not know Proverbs 3:5-6 that states to trust in the Lord with all thine heart; and lean not unto thine own understanding. In all thy ways acknowledge Him, and He shall direct thy paths. He had no knowledge that the fear of the Lord is the beginning of wisdom (Proverbs 9:10).

Yet, Noah had such fear, such awe, such reverence, such respect for God that he did not lean upon his own understanding about what God had warned. Listen to me, Noah did not even know what a flood was.

> For the Lord God had not caused it to rain upon the earth, and there was not a man to till the ground. But there went up a mist from the earth, and watered the whole face of the ground (Genesis 2:5b-6).

That did not matter to Noah, for he walked with God. He was a man who had communion with God; he talked and conversed with God. Godlike faith doesn't question what God says, it obeys.

Noah exhibited Godlike faith amidst a wicked and perverse generation. He kept himself separate from the moral evil of the society around him. He was willing to be mocked and laughed at by those around him. Noah was not looking to be popular or accepted by the crowd. He didn't care what people thought of him. Building his ark was his goal and He endeavored to build it to God's exact dimensions.

I can state that, because it is obvious that if Noah had been concerned if he was liked by others, he would not have built the ark where everyone thought he was bonkers. I mean, who builds an ark in the desert with no means of getting it to water? Can we imagine what it must have looked like. A man claiming that a flood is about to destroy all living souls. He had to seem a fool, for it was not only Noah that never heard or seen such a thing. None of the people had any idea of what he was describing.

> And spared not the old world, but saved Noah the eighth person, a preacher of righteousness, bringing in the flood upon the world of the ungodly (2 Peter 2:5).

Here we see that Noah was not only building the ark, but was a preacher of righteousness. That means that amongst all the immorality prevailing in his day, Noah was steadfast in proclaiming morality.

There was in his day the necessity for an extraordinary Divine judgment. The long-lived lives of his day proved to be immense in its sins and abominations that God had to remove them. But God never lets His judgment fall without first giving sufficient warning and providing opportunity for repentance.

Before we think that this is straying from Godlike faith, let's understand that all of what Noah did was exhibiting such faith. He was not only to warn by word, but he was to warn by his life and actions. His daily building the ark and his daily testifying of his belief in the Divine warning were his Godlike faith in action.

Let's look at the extent of Noah's faith. God had warned Noah of the flood, or of a great judgment unheard of at that time. It was something that they had never seen. There was no evidence of such. It was unheard of, it sounded ridiculous. I mean, rain and then a flood.

> Now faith is the substance of things hoped for, the evidence of things not seen (Hebrews 11:1).

Yet, Noah acted upon faith. He trusted God so fully that he believed what was not seen. He had a firm conviction in that which he heard from God. Although he had never seen rain or a flood, that didn't matter. Noah trusted that because God promised a flood, He would bring it to pass.

Noah didn't try to understand what a flood was. He didn't think logically about what God meant. He didn't ask God to explain rain and a flood. Noah took God at His Word and obeyed. How many of us just obey?

God told him to build an ark and warn others of the coming judgment. Noah obeys and starts building a large vessel. A structure such as had never been seen by man from the foundation of the world. Can we imagine the cost of such an endeavor. Noah probably exhausted every bit of pecuniary that he possessed. Plus, it took about one-hundred years to build it.

> And let us not be weary in well doing: for in due season we shall reap, if we faint not (Galatians 6:9).

How many of us have that kind of stick-to-itiveness? Let's face it, that was a long time for Noah to not give up. While he was building the ark, busy about well doing, at his own expense and labor, men scoffed at him. We can imagine that people must have called him a deluded prophet, a foolish dreamer, etc.

However, things have not changed. As people were in Noah's day, they exist in our day. Today, if we endeavor to do something for the Lord that others don't believe or that seems farfetched, we are called a religious fanatic, a religious radical, a maniac, a spiritual nut, an extremist, etc.

At this time, I want to interject a story that happened to me years ago concerning how doing God's will can initiate ridicule. I mean when God tells you to do something that you don't understand. Anyway, I was pastoring a church and I was directed by the Lord to speak to a woman in the congregation. God wanted me to warn her that He didn't want her son to start his senior year in the town they lived in. She stared at me and started to laugh. I was accused of joking because it would not be right to take her son away from all his friends that he grew up with in his last year of school. A few weeks went by and the Lord impressed me to go to her again. When I did, she was quite annoyed with me and told me that she had made up her mind that she would not put her son through such anxiety. She stared at me and firmly stated that God would not do something so heartless. Of course, she was insinuating that I was lying.

By this time, I am seeking the Lord about the situation. I was beginning to feel somewhat foolish. However, about a week later, He sent me again. This time, I was adamant that she listen to the Lord's word. She laughed at me and told me that I took things too seriously and accused me of being too zealous. She claimed that she had discussed this with the Lord and they will move after her son graduates.

At any rate, my daughters and I had stopped by her house the day that her son started his senior year. She smiled and said that they would be looking to move after he graduated. About two hours after we left her house, I received a call from a local pastor who was a friend. He told me that she had been brutally murdered.

The other point about this story is that the Lord had told me a year earlier to tell her that she was wrong in letting her son be friends with a boy who obviously was not a Christian. At that time, she informed me that they had been friends since first grade and the boy was like a second son to her. I proceeded to tell her that I believe that the Lord wants her to stop him from coming to her house and stop her son from staying at his house. She smiled, shook her head, and said that I have to loosen up about things. Besides their friendship isn't like being yoked in marriage. I told her that their friendship was an unequal yoke. Anyway, she just laughed, shook her head, and gestured with her hands.

Yes, it was that boy who was like a son that slit her throat and stabbed her seventeen times. He was into some sort of Satan worship. Apparently, he hated his father and wanted to practice killing someone before murdering his father. I know that this is a tough story, for it was a difficult time for me. But I pray that it helps us to realize that Godlike faith will be mocked, ridiculed, and humiliated. Like Noah, we must not be concerned if we are liked. It is our responsibility to obey God, even if they don't heed the warning.

Let's get back to Noah. Genesis 6:8 states that Noah found grace in the eyes of the Lord. Yet, when God examined the hearts of all other men at that time, it was in Noah that He found that one essential factor that set him apart from the rest. Noah had faith. He loved God more than the wickedness the men of that day loved. They worshipped the lusts of the flesh, the lusts of the eyes, the pride of life, and looked to please self. Noah loved righteousness and looked to please God.

What does Hebrews 11:7 mean by its claim that Noah condemned the world? Let's think about that. Noah heard from God, he believed God, built an ark to the saving of his house, and condemned the world. That means that because Noah lived the life of faith before the world, his witness condemned them. During the one-hundred years that he was engaged in building the ark, he preached righteousness with earnestness and fidelity. Although his preaching would condemn them, it was the example of his life that truly condemned them.

What we have to understand is that his faith condemned their unbelief. His fear or respect of God condemned their lack of fear or respect. His obedience condemned their disobedience. Even if Noah had not continuously preached about the coming judgment, his constructing the ark would have been a continual reproof to those ignoring the warning.

Because the world had plenty of warning from Noah's preaching and his life lived, they would have no excuse before God. Since Noah's life condemned their life, God would be justified in His judgment. The question here is whether or not our life is condemning the wickedness of the world. Are we separate from them? Does our life reflect Jesus or self? What does our life produce? Is it the works of the flesh or the Fruit of the Spirit? Are we more concerned about pleasing people than pleasing God?

Now, Noah knew that God was going to send judgment on those around him that did not love the Lord, so he kept building the ark to make sure that he and his house were not part of the judgment. That is what we are supposed to do. We are promised that the salvation of our house is offered to our family if we believe on the Lord Jesus Christ. We need to be mindful to keep building the ark for them to enter. It is a daily building and a daily warning of the judgment to come. We have to love our family enough to warn them of the consequences of their sin. If we condone their adultery, fornication, lying, etc., don't want to hurt their feelings, are concerned that they will hate us, we are keeping them from the ark of safety.

Let's focus on this differently, for I believe that God wants us to see more in this chapter. Noah was a man who walked with God and possessed Godlike faith. A man who believed what God said without any visible evidence. It was something unheard of and never seen.

A man or woman that possesses Godlike faith, believes the word of God, and does not question it. It doesn't matter if we have never seen such a thing, ever heard of such a thing, or whether we understand what He is telling us to do. God said it and that's all that matters to us.

Let me explain Godlike faith. Some of us have been promised things. Yes, we do not see them and some promises seem unbelievable. However, just because we don't see it, doesn't count. God sees it and that is all that matters. Remember our promise our answered prayer is in Heaven the moment the promise was given and the moment that we prayed the prayer of faith.

God is able to bring about what He sees even if we can't see it. He wants us to go about building our ark, keep busy with well doing, doing the will of God, and He will bring about the promise right in the middle of our well doing. We must realize that Godlike faith believes and doesn't stand around looking for the promise. To do so, would mean that we are not building our ark, but standing idly by.

What does it mean to build our ark? Let's look at Noah to help us understand. God warned Noah of the coming judgment, He then tells him to build the ark, and it had to be built according to God's standards. If it was done as God commanded or instructed, it would be the salvation of Noah and his family. In other words, they would be protected or saved from the coming judgment. That is Godlike faith in action. Hearing from God, obeying God, and following His parameters.

We build our ark to keep ourselves and our family from the coming judgment in the same manner as Noah. No, it is not a physical structure. Our ark is spiritual and must adhere to God's standards. That means that as we serve God according to His word, we are building that ark of protection for ourselves and our family.

Too many Christians do not realize that following the world, loving the things of the world, and compromising His Word is not building our ark according to God's requirements. Our carnal ark will not save us or our family. In *Storms Are Faith's Workout,* I spoke about how Christian parents are compromising God's word and the consequences of such concession to their children.

Now, Noah didn't know the time of the flood. All he knew is that he had to build the ark and nothing could deviate him from his task. He was continuously busy about the commission that God gave him. Godlike faith is not sidetracked by anyone or anything. It focuses on God and His assignment. Such faith knows that whatever God tells us to do will never go against His written word. Even if we have read it in the Bible, but have never literally seen it, we do it.

We reap in His due season. God alone knows the season that He will fulfill His promise of saving our loved ones. Keeping our eyes on the awaited promise will keep us away from building our ark. We stay busy about building according to God's word and let God take care of His promise. If we want it fulfilled, we had better be busy with what He has told us to do. We construct the ark and God will see that they enter. However, if we are compromising His standards for them, He is not our God. They are.

I sense that God is about to bring about the due season in some of our lives. We have been arduously building our ark for ourselves and our family. We have received much ridicule by those that we love. Sometimes we have felt weary, but the salvation of ourselves and our family from the coming judgment kept us steadfastly building. Only Godlike faith knows that Satan has no authority over us. Thus, we will overcome all obstacles that would try to sway us from building our ark!

Chapter 9

Godlike Faith Discerns God's Voice

> And he came thither unto a cave, and lodged there; and, behold, the word of the Lord came to him, and he said unto him, What doest thou here, Elijah? And he said, I have been very jealous for the Lord God of Hosts: for the children of Israel have forsaken thy covenant, thrown down thine altars, and slain thy prophets with the sword; and I, even I only, am left; and they seek my life, to take it away. And he said, go forth, and stand upon the mount before the Lord. And, behold, the Lord passed by, and a great and strong wind rent the mountains, and brake in pieces the rocks before the Lord; but the Lord was not in the wind: and after the wind an earthquake; but the Lord was not in the earthquake; and after the earthquake a fire; but the Lord was not in the fire: And after the fire a still small voice (1 Kings 19:9-12).

> My sheep hear my voice, and I know them, and they follow me (John 10:27).

> And a stranger will they not follow, but will flee from him: for they know not the voice of strangers (John 10:5).

According to the scriptures above, we will see that some of us might be looking for the voice of God or the will of God in the *wind,* the *earthquake,* or the *fire.* In other words, we are not sure what God's voice is. Yet, Jesus states in John 10:27 that the voice of God is known and heard by His sheep. This is a promise. Yet, it seems to be so unfulfilled in the lives of many in the Church today.

I don't know how many have said to me that they do not know the voice of God. Others say it with such anger and claim that God won't talk to me. Some claim that they hear something, but don't know if it's God or not.

Let me make clear that if we are God's child, He talks to us. It is no fault on God's behalf, but a failure on our part. We spend too much time listening to the voice of self, and the voices that are contrary to the voice of God. We have no one to blame but ourselves. When we realize that truth, we will stop thinking that God doesn't love me, God doesn't talk to me, etc. I mean, really what godly parent doesn't love or talk to their child? God is the perfect Father.

What most of us have not learned or understood is the voice of God goes contrary to what we really want to do and to hear. Thus, we claim that we want to hear God. But when He speaks, we listen to the voice of the *wind*, the *earthquake*, or the *fire*, and don't hear Him.

We must comprehend that there are many voices in the world today. We have the voice of the media we hear, the television we watch, the radio we listen to, the newspaper and the books we read, etc. Furthermore, there are the voices of dignitaries that rule our city, state, and federal government. We have the voices of our peers, whether family, friends, business associates, etc.

In short, there is the voice of enticement all around us. These voices beckon us to come. They cry so loudly telling us to live while we can, you only go this round once, you owe it to yourself to enjoy what little time there is in this life. Then there are other voices of the New Age steering us to worship self which is idolatry. We can readily hear the voices of false prophets who are preachers of itching ears. These voices appeal to our flesh that loves pleasures and loves to pamper its wants.

There so many loud clamoring voices demanding us to follow. They are constantly telling us to do this, don't do that, what to believe, what not to believe, etc. These bombarding voices can begin to weigh us down with their screaming and demanding us to follow.

Now, finally there is the voice of God and His ministers (not itching ear preachers) who are also the voice of God. His voice is the only voice of truth. But because of the thunderous voices, many don't know how to discern the voice of God. They are confused about how to know God's voice.

When Elijah was running from Jezebel, he found that God's voice wasn't in the strong wind, it wasn't in the earthquake, and it wasn't in the fire. It was the still small voice.

Let's understand that is a major key. The other voices are loud and ringing in our ears. They are pushy and try to shove us in their direction. These try to appear as mighty and powerful so that we listen to them.

The majority are like that. When we try to answer biblically, they accuse us of being too religious or accuse us of judging. They do anything to persuade us to their way of thinking. In doing so many have become hearers only of God's word. Then we wonder why we don't know God's voice. How can we, when we are listening to all those demanding voices?

If we want to know and hear God's voice, we have to wait for the whispering voice. It is a gentle dove that will not overpower us. The other voices will beat at us until they rule over our own will.

God has given us a free will. We have the freedom of choice to choose whose voice we will listen to. God will not overstep our will to do His will. God will not force us to do what is right. We must overstep our selfish, self-centered will to listen to Him.

To help us understand His voice, we will look more closely at the voices of the wind, the earthquake, and the fire.

The voice of the Wind

> That we henceforth be no more children, tossed to and fro, and carried about with every wind of doctrine by the sleight of men, and cunning craftiness, whereby they lie in wait to deceive (Ephesians 4:14).

The voice of the wind takes hold of us and sways us until we are so tossed about that we don't know what is up from what is down. We begin to question what is right or wrong. Our mind is in a state of confusion. It is like a whirlwind that has us all discombobulated.

As we listen to this doctrine, that teaching, read this book, etc., New Age teaching starts to sound reasonable. Compromising our Christian principles or stand for the sake of friends or family sounds like a reasonable doctrine. Besides we don't want to offend them or they will never listen to us. So, we offend Christ and the Gospel.

All of a sudden, just like a strong wind, our morals have swayed from doing only what glorifies God to what pleases the majority or self. In other words, we become so disoriented from this tossing to and fro, that we no longer walk in stability. Our feet are no longer planted on that solid foundation. The rock that we once stood on has become sand which leads to a great fall.

The voice of the Earthquake

> Be merciful unto me, O God: for man would swallow me up; he fighting daily oppresseth me. Mine enemies would daily swallow me up: for they be many that fight against me, O thou most high. What time I am afraid, I will trust in thee (Psalm 56:1-3).

We have all seen earthquakes in a movie, on the news, etc. It swallows up all that's around. Well, the voice of the earthquake tries to swallow us up, until we are imprisoned in its desires, its abyss, its void, its depth, its vacuum, its chasm.

Listen to me, the voice of the earthquake comes so fast that we don't realize what is happening until it's too late. We are walking steady and seem to be in control. The next thing we know, we are shaken and swallowed up before we realized what was going on. Sort of like Eve who was walking in the Garden and the next moment, she is cast out of it.

Once swallowed up by the earthquake, we are buried along with our pleasures. They can't help us now. Those pleasures for a season are no longer pleasures, but the means of our destruction.

The voice of the Fire

For wickedness burneth as the fire (Isaiah 9:18).

The voice of the fire inflames, it incites, it stimulates, it burns, etc. When I hear words like that, I think of the passions. Passions are appetites, obsessions, desires, cravings, hungers lusts, etc.

Now, what are the passions or lusts or fires of this natural life? They are the lusts of the flesh, the lusts of the eyes, and the pride of life (1 John 2:16). The voice of fire is the one that gets a hold of us until we are consumed by our passions and the lusts of the flesh will burn us up.

Let me explain this more clearly. As we listen to the voice of the fire, we begin to take on the mentality of the world. We think what is wrong with a little petting or a little necking? What's wrong with a little drugs, a little pornography, a little illicit sex, etc.? I mean, how many are claiming to be a Christian and are committing the sins of adultery, fornication, etc., that will not enter Heaven, and believe that it's okay since we love each other? Because of the lusts of our flesh, we have blatantly sinned against God. We are to love Him and keep his commandments. To sin against God's word means that we have chosen to love self and not God.

The voice of the fire shouts at our passions. After all, the Bible says that God created all things good. We can go overboard with this religious stuff. Before long, our conscience is so seared, so burnt up by our passions that we see nothing wrong with sin and are indulging in the cup of our lusts.

The voice of fire proclaims that premarital sex is a way to show you care for a boyfriend or girlfriend. An extra marital affair keeps the boredom out of marriage. A little pot is good for the nerves.

If we listen to the voice of fire, it will incite wicked passions. It convinces us that a little pornography stimulates so we can feel more like a man or woman. We feel that our nerves are shattered, so the pot is so soothing.

A sad truth is that the voice of fire is burning people alive. Sin is not only in the world, but it is consuming the Church. In many cases, we can't tell the Christian from the unsaved. Both look alike, talk alike, have the same vices or sins.

Why is this happening? Because the Christian doesn't know the voice of God. The other voices are so prominent. We are not waiting on God and we are not listening to God. Until we stand against the voice of the wind, the voice of the earthquake, and the voice of the fire, we will never hear the still small voice of God.

It is through these voices that Satan is taking power or authority over Christians. He doesn't have any authority over us, so he uses our fleshly appetites against us. If we have not learned to walk in Godlike faith, they will overpower us.

We have to learn self-control through allowing the Holy Spirit to have His way in our life. As we do that, we understand that the voice of God is not the loud one in the crowd. It is easier on our flesh to hear those clamoring voices of wind, earthquake, and fire. These voices speak so thunderous and so clear to the old nature. We can only hear the voice of God as we still our flesh. In other words, deny it place.

Jesus said that His sheep know His voice, follow His voice, and do not know the voice of a stranger, and will not follow a stranger. Yet, for too many in the Church, the stranger that we are not following is Jesus. It is the voice of Jesus that is the stranger to many of God's soldiers.

Why is this happening? It is quite simple; we are not following His word. Too many listen to whatever, whoever, and never or very seldom ever read our Bible to learn His voice. How can we discern His voice when we don't obey His word? If we cannot obey His word in the small things, then we will not obey His word in the big things.

GODLIKE FAITH DISCERNS GOD'S VOICE

Let me explain this. God's word says to do something and we don't. Instead, we decide to do something else. While doing the opposite of what we were told to do, we heard the quickening of the Holy Spirit warning us. But we felt it was the right thing to do, so we ignored the Holy Spirit and did it anyway.

Whether or not our motive seemed good, God's word must be obeyed in all things. It must be listened to in all things. If we make excuses for our sin and disobey God's word and the Holy Spirit's prompting, our conscience will become calloused. When that happens only the loud voices of the wind, earthquake, and fire will penetrate.

This chapter is necessary for us to learn God's voice. Godlike faith can never be cultivated in our life until His children discern and hear His voice. All other voices will lead to sin and possible shipwreck. Only knowing and obeying the voice of God will we have the faith that gives no place to Satan.

Yes, the voice of God is not pleasing to our flesh. It is harder to hear. Remember when Jesus had said unless ye eat of the flesh of the Son of Man and drink his blood, ye have no life in you (John 6:53). Many of His disciples claimed that it was a hard saying; who can hear it? After that many of them went back, and walked no more with Him (John 6:60,66).

What I believe the Lord wants us to understand is that much of what the voice of God has to say is a hard saying on our flesh. To discern and hear His voice means that we are willing to hear correction, rebuke, instruction, etc. whatever is hard on our old nature. It is cultivated by being willing to hear God say no to something that we really want. Without truly learning to deny self, we will always listen to the loud voices that drown out the still small voice of God.

Some of us are wondering what discerning the voice of God has to do with Godlike faith. It has much to do with it. Jesus is our example of overcoming this life through faith. He did always only those things that please the Father (John 8:29). We know that only faith pleases God (Hebrews 11:6). Jesus was led by the Holy Spirit. In other words, the only voice that He followed was the voice of

God. Godlike faith is developed through following only God's voice. It doesn't hear the voices of wind, earthquake, and fire that will lead astray or cause us to go shipwreck.

That kind of faith can only come about as we willingly deny our self whatever it wants. As John the Baptist said, "He must increase, but I must decrease" (John 3:30). He cannot increase, unless we keep under our body and bring it into submission to the will of God (1 Corinthians 9:27). Our old nature wants to be the boss, but in Christianity, it must always be the servant. That means that many hard sayings of truth will not rest easy on us, if we are not dead to self and alive to Christ.

Only as we are zealous to listen to the hard sayings from the voice of God will the voices of the wind, earthquake, and fire become lower and lower and lower. As that happens, that still small voice of the Lord will become louder and louder and louder until we become deaf to the voices of the wind, earthquake, and fire. Then the only voice that Godlike faith hears and follows is the voice of God and the other voices become strangers that we no longer listen to!

Chapter 10

Godlike Faith Does Not Fear

And I said unto you, Ye are come unto the mountain of the Amorites, which the Lord our God doth give unto us. Behold, the Lord thy God hath set the land before thee: go up and possess it, as the Lord God of thy fathers hath said unto thee; fear not, neither be discouraged . . . Notwithstanding ye would not go up, but rebelled against the commandment of the Lord your God . . . The Lord your God which goeth before you, he shall fight for you, according to all that he did for you in Egypt before your eyes . . . Yet in this thing ye did not believe the Lord your God, Who went in the way before you, to search you out a place to pitch your tents in, in fire by night, to shew you by what way ye should go, and in a cloud by day (Deuteronomy 1:20-33).

For God hath not given us the spirit of fear; but of power, and of love, and of a sound mind (2 Timothy 1:7).

For ye have not received the spirit of bondage again to fear; but ye have received the Spirit of adoption, whereby we cry, Abba, Father (Romans 8:15).

THE verses in deuteronomy refer to the Israelites not entering the land that God had promised at their first arrival at Kadesh-Barnea. We all know this story of the ten doubting spies giving an evil report and the two faith filled spies (Joshua and Caleb) giving a righteous report.

Because of the ten faithless, doubting spies, Israel rebelled against God's command to go in and take the land. Although we all know this story, we need to take a closer look as to why this took place.

For this, we look at Deuteronomy 1:28: Whither shall we go up? Our brethren have discouraged our heart, saying, The people is greater and taller than we; the cities are great and walled up to heaven; and moreover we have seen the sons of the Anakims there.

As I meditated upon that verse, the words discouraged our heart, walled up to heaven, and the sons of the Anakims stood out to me. When I read the words, "whither shall we go up" it made no sense to me, but the words, "walled up to heaven" made me think. So, I did some research and discovered that these fortified walls were common in the area and are still there even today.

For instance, the Monastery on Mt. Sinai is surrounded with very high walls without any gate. In the upper part of the wall is a sort of window or opening from which a basket is suspended by a pulley. That is the means whereby both people and goods are received and sent from the place.

Apparently, the Israelites had never before seen such walls or fortifications. So, that helped me to understand why they asked how they were to go up. How would they get up such walls?

Then to top it off, they saw the Sons of the Anakims there. This was a race of giants that dwelled in the southern part of Canaan. Their war like appearance struck the Israelites with terror.

Now, let's concentrate on the words, "our brethren have discouraged our heart." We want to focus our attention on the word "discouraged." The Hebrew word means to faint with fear, to melt away, to liquify. Oxford dictionary says if we are discouraged, we are without courage or confidence.

What the word discouraged means is that our brethren have caused us to be without confidence or to have no confidence. Yet, further contemplation on this verse revealed that this is an example of fear overcoming faith.

Let's look at the definition of fear. It is defined as a panic that grips a person causing him to run away, be alarmed, scared, frightened, dismayed, filled with dread, intimidated, anxious, and apprehensive.

> Be not afraid of sudden fear, neither of the desolation of the wicked, when it cometh. For the Lord shall be thy confidence, and shall keep thy foot from being taken (Proverbs 3:25-26).

Deuteronomy stated that they were discouraged or without confidence. When they listened to or believed the lies of the faithless ten spies, it caused them to become faithless. They were over wrought with fear and lost confidence.

I said that it was fear overcoming faith. Perhaps, a better way of putting it is unbelief, a lack of confidence in God and His ability to do as He promised overruled faith and trust in God and His ability to do as He promised.

Their discouraged heart meant that they feared the enemy and had no confidence in the God who had shown Himself mighty in Egypt, the miraculous crossing of the Red Sea, etc.

Then I thought about how many times Christians receive a mandate or a promise from the Lord and then let others, whether Christians or the world, persuade us to do otherwise. They cause us to question if we have really heard from God, question if that is really what the Lord meant, question if we may be too spiritual, etc. On the other hand, it may seem like it is never going to become a reality as we wait and wait and wait for the promise.

Whatever it is that causes the discouragement of heart, our lack of confidence in God will always cause us to yield to a spirit of fear. We may quote 2 Timothy 1:7 that God has not given us a spirit of fear. However the hurling questions and doubts cause us to become fearful.

The fear in 2 Timothy in the Greek implies a spirit to be timid, to dread, to be faithless, to be fearful. But before we look further into this verse to reveal what God wants us to come out of this chapter with, we will look at Romans 8:15 of our opening Scripture texts.

Bondage in the Greek means to be a slave to; to serve. The fear in those verses means to be put in fear, alarm, fright, terror. It states that we are not a slave to serve fear, fright, or terror. We have been delivered from such because we are a child of God.

> There is no fear in love; but perfect love casteth out fear: because fear hath torment. He that feareth is not made perfect in love (1 John 4:18).

If we love God with our whole being, with everything, we will not fear anyone or anything. We must understand that perfect love trusts God, believes that all things work together for good. That means that we rest in God, even when we don't understand a bit of it (like Noah). We know God and His word, and that is all that matters.

Thus, we are no longer a slave to serve fear. We serve love. Love for God casts out fear, because we have confidence in God's love for us. We trust Him no matter what is going on. It is like the three Hebrew boys. We believe that God is able to deliver us from the fiery furnace, if not, we will not serve fear.

Okay, let's look back at 2 Timothy 1:7 to see what spirit God has given us. It is the Spirit of power, and of love, and of a sound mind. A Spirit of power in the Greek means the power to work miracles, power to confound enemies, power to support us in trials, and the power to enable us to do that which is lawful and right in His sight.

A Spirit of love means the love which enables us to believe, hope, and endure all things. It is the ability to love the loveless as Jesus does. Through His love we can stand up against the persecution, hatred, and condemnation of the world.

The Spirit of a sound mind means a clear understanding, a sound judgment, a refined or purified will, holy passions, heavenly tempers. In other words, it is the whole soul completely regulated and influenced by the Holy Spirit to think, to speak, and to act rightly in all things. In short, to have a Spirit of a sound mind is to be led by the Holy Spirit in all things. It is to have the mind of Christ.

So, God has given us the Spirit of power to work miracles, to confound enemies, to support us in trials. The Spirit of love that enables us to believe, hope, and endure all things. The Spirit of a sound mind enables us to have a clear understanding, sound judgment, and heavenly temper enabling us to think, speak and act right in all things.

God has not given us the spirit of fear or the spirit of bondage to fear. But as the Israelites in our Scripture text, are we looking at the walls fortified to Heaven and the giants that make us look like grasshoppers. Are we allowing our circumstances, our work, our families, our finances, etc. to appear as if they are unscalable? Do we believe that we can never climb over them?

Has unbelief in God's word, His promises caused us to see the problem as a Giant and our faith in God as a grasshopper? If we continue to believe the lies of doubt, fear will rise up in our heart. If that happens, we will find ourselves in the place of the Israelites where faith turns into unbelief. Once our heart becomes discouraged, our confidence in God, in His word, and in His ability will decrease as the walls of our problems increase.

Fear caused the Israelites to distrust God. Doubt caused them to believe that the God who gave them a mighty deliverance from Egypt, who caused the Red Sea to part and allow them to walk on dry land, etc. could not see them through to the promise. This same fear caused them to believe that the God who spoke all things into existence had somehow become impotent and no longer omnipotent. He who is all powerful had through their fear and unbelief become powerless.

The interior counsel of their heart elicited by the exterior lies of the ten unbelieving spies caused them to question what they had been told or promised by God. Whether it is the doubting Thomas, the long wait, or whatever, we must not give into the fear that will try desperately to cause us to doubt God. If we question God, we will lose confidence in the only One who can deliver His promise.

Satan knows that if he can get us to fear, he has authority or power over us, and our next step is unbelief. When that happens, God is prevented from keeping His promise to us.

> But without faith it is impossible to please him: for he that cometh to God must believe that he is, and that he is a rewarder of them that diligently seek him (Hebrews 11:6).
>
> And let us not be weary in well doing: for in due season we shall reap, if we faint not (Galatians 6:9).

God has not given us a spirit of fear. We are not slaves to serve fear. For He has given us the Spirit of power to work miracles, to confound the enemies, to support us in trials. We have been given the Spirit of love that enables us to believe, to hope, and to endure all things. He has given us the Spirit of a sound mind to have a clear understanding, sound judgment, and heavenly temper enabling us to think, to speak, and to act according to His will in all things.

Why is it important to understand that Godlike faith doesn't fear? What is fear? It is defined as a panic that grips us causing us to run away, be alarmed, scared, frightened, dismayed, filled with dread, intimidated, anxious, and apprehensive.

Fear has devastating results. It can virtually paralyze us and make us helpless. When fear takes hold, it stops the flow of God's power. Fear is unbelief in action. It is a spiritual power and force that we need to bind and command away in the Name of Jesus (Matthew 18:18).

We must understand that fear is a dark shadow that surrounds us and ultimately imprisons us within ourselves. Each of us has been a prisoner of fear at one time or another with fear of rejection, fear of misunderstanding, fear of uncertainty, fear of sickness, fear of the unknown, fear of the dark, or even fear of death.

But God has not given us a spirit of fear. He has given us that which is necessary to overcome any fear the devil may try to overpower us with. Jesus possessed Godlike faith and nothing that Satan came at Him with caused Him to fear. He knew His Father was greater than any weapon of the enemy and He stood firm in His knowledge of God and His ability.

That's what God wants us to understand in this chapter. Fear is a tool or power of the devil. Christ has given us power and authority over all Satan's power. So, when the devil comes at us with His tactics of fear, we stand fully armed in God's armor and face him in Godlike faith. When he sees that we are standing in the power of Christ, he has to flee!

Chapter 11

Godlike Faith Plants a Good Crop

> Be not deceived; God is not mocked: for whatsoever a man soweth, that shall he also reap (Galatians 6:7).

THIS chapter is going to show Godlike faith in a different perspective. It is to reveal that every thought we think is sowing or planting a crop. Christians are being overtaken by crops or harvests that are discouraging, destroying, confusing, etc.

We can't understand why this is happening or that is happening in our life. It makes no sense when the word of God says differently. We know the word and yet what we are reaping is not what the Lord promises in Scripture.

However, we continue to sow or plant more negativity, lack of faith, fleshly, carnal minded seeds that are yielding crops. Galatians plainly states that what we sow is what we reap. How do we think that we can sow or plant a certain seed and harvest or receive a different crop? If we think that, we are deceived.

James 1:22 tells us to be doers of the word and not hearers only deceiving our own selves. To be deceived in the Greek means to delude or beguile our self.

Many Christians are reaping or harvesting crops of sickness, disease, debt, lack, anger, frustrations, stress, etc. Why is that? Because of the seed we have planted.

Let's understand how we plant wrong seed season after season.

> Because the carnal mind is enmity against God: for it is not subject to the law of God, neither indeed can be. So then they that are in the flesh cannot please God (Romans 8:7-8).

The problem is that the flesh, the carnal mind, the nonspiritual thinking is the nature that we were born with. It's like a comfortable set of clothes. There is no discomfort. It feels so natural. However, as a Christian, we are to put on the new suit, new apparel that is called the new man in Christ (Ephesians 4:22-24).

Righteousness and holiness are completely opposite of the flesh or the carnal mind. Our flesh or carnal mind tries to convince us that we owe it to ourselves to indulge it, to satisfy it. The flesh revels in the lusts of the flesh, the lusts of the eyes, and the pride of life (1 John 2:16). That is the deeds or works of the flesh. But God says that we owe the flesh nothing and owe Him what we cannot ever pay (Romans 8:12-13).

Yet, we continuously sow seeds of gossip, pride, gluttony, defiling the temple of the Holy Ghost (our body), negative thoughts, wrong or wicked thoughts, worry, anxiety, jealousy, fear, arguing, immorality, lack of respect for those we are to honor, or all seeds contrary to God's word.

We must comprehend how vital it is to our spiritual wellbeing to control what we sow or what we plant. Because if we think that we can reap God's blessings or His promises when we are sowing seeds that reap the opposite, we are deceived.

How many times have we sang that God will make a way where there seems to be no way? I thought about that and how we think of Israel standing at the Red Sea fearing for their life and Moses saying: "Fear ye not, stand still, and see the salvation of the Lord, which he will shew to you today: for the Egyptians whom ye have seen today, ye shall see them again no more for ever (Exodus 14:13).

I believe that we tend to just stand there or stay in our situation and wait for fire to come down from Heaven or something. We are looking for God to do something. But God wants us to understand that it is our seeds planted that have caused our situation. He has had no part in our planting. Our seed sown is what we have reaped.

The verses in Ephesians 4:22-24 told us to put off our former conversation or conduct, be renewed in the spirit of our mind, and put on the new man. Our mind is our mental inclination, our purpose, our mind set. It is that which we think.

Why is it necessary to be renewed in our mind or to change the way we think? Because God is and has been trying to get us to change our thinking so that we can change our crop. We must see, our negative thinking is the negative seeds that we have been working overtime to sow or plant. Then we are overwhelmed by our sin, sickness, disease, poverty, lack, gossip, etc. that is destroying us.

We feel something and immediately think that we may have this or have that. If we feel out of sorts, we think that we have the flu or something. If a bill comes in and we know that we have missed work because of sickness, we think that we will have our car repossessed.

It is not God's fault that we are not reaping or harvesting righteousness, health, wealth, abundance, pure thoughts of others, or the overflowing of His blessings and promises. But what is the way of escape from all this negative overflow in our life?

> Let this mind be in you, which was also in Christ Jesus (Philippians 2:5).

If we allow the thinking, the direction, the understanding of Christ to be ours, we will never think or meditate on worry, fear, anxiety, finances, food, etc. The way to escape the overflow of bad crops is to *immediately* start planting the word of God, faith in God, positive thoughts, and then our crop overflow will be what God wills for us. In other words, we have to train our thinking to be opposite of our flesh. If we feel something, we need to think that we were healed at Calvary. When the bill comes in, we think that God will supply all our need. We have to train our thoughts to be in line with Scriptures. Then when we are confronted with something, we will not plant negative thoughts according to the flesh, but plant positive thoughts of the word of God.

Our mind is the planting ground. It is where we bury the seeds that will sprout forth. We must not be deceived in this. Whatever seed we sow or plant is what we will reap, receive a crop of, or harvest. As God spoke the worlds into existence, our thoughts bring forth the crop in our life.

Okay, let's think about a harvest field. It is large, a great crop, or plentiful bounty. Now, if you realize that you don't want that crop, you tear it up. Then immediately sow or plant what you want to harvest.

If we can start to see this process of sowing (planting) and reaping (the harvest or crop), we can instantly say, "NO." I don't want this crop. I destroy the seed and will plant the seed that will yield me the crop that I desire. We must recognize that we are thinking that which is opposite of what we truly want to reap. I want to say that again. It is time that we comprehend that we are dwelling on thoughts (planting seeds) that we truly don't want to harvest.

We must plant positive, faith in God and His word seeds. If we do that, we will yield the blessing and the promises of God. When negative thoughts of fear, doubt, worry, frustration, wrong desires, etc. try to plant themselves, we must straightway destroy the seed and plant positive thoughts of faith. We must quote His promises and plant them in the fertile ground of faith.

Then our harvest or that which we reap will be an overflow and abundance of righteousness, health, wealth, God's fruit of love, joy, peace, longsuffering, gentleness, goodness, faith, meekness, and temperance (self-control).

Again, Jesus is our example of Godlike faith. He never allowed any negative thoughts, etc. to enter His mind. His reaping was always the will of God. Never did He have to pull up a crop and replant. We have a way out of our bad crop. It is through changing the way we think. As soon as we change the way we think from negative to positive, we have planted a good crop!

Chapter 12

Godlike Faith is of the Spirit

> Wherefore I put thee in remembrance that thou stir up the gift of God, which is in thee by the putting on of my hands. For God hath not given us the spirit of fear, but of power, and of love, and of a sound mind. Be not thou therefore ashamed of the testimony of our Lord, nor of me his prisoner: but be thou partaker of the afflictions of the gospel according to the power of God; Who hath saved us, and called us with an holy calling, not according to our works, but according to his own purpose and grace, which was given us in Christ Jesus before the world began (2 Timothy 1:6-9).

ALTHOUGH this chapter touches upon fear, it is meant to reveal the real character of Christianity. As it is imparted into our souls and becomes part of our life, it is generally misunderstood. In other words, once the divine nature becomes part of our life and is evidenced, it is usually misjudged.

Why is that so? Because it forms a man or woman of energy. It operates like a new creation. This energy or better called Holy Ghost zeal changes us to a very considerable extent. Our views, dispositions, habits, friends, desires, etc. change so much that we no longer seem to be the same person.

In fact, if we allow the gift within us to be stirred up or become active in our life, we are transformed into the divine image in righteousness and true holiness. What that means is that if we continue to allow the gift of the Holy Spirit to have His way, we will be transformed from the image of fallen man into the image of the new man created in Christ.

We become like Jesus in this world. As Jesus feared nothing, His disciples fear nothing. However, in our text there is the implication that Timothy was not letting the Holy Spirit stir up his soul. It appears by Paul's words that he was afraid and ashamed.

Let's make this clear, Paul was rebuking Timothy. Yes, it was done in love, but it was a rebuke, nonetheless. Furthermore, it is a rebuke to any of us found in his situation.

We sense that Timothy was of a timid personality and was being influenced by the Jews and false teachers around him. It seems that he was afraid to speak out against wrongs or sin, and he was ashamed of the fact that Paul was in prison. How many today are afraid to name sin as sin?

Timothy, through fear, was neglectful of his duty. It was his responsibility to love enough to tell the truth. He was to give the word of God whether or not it was accepted by the hearers. Scripture makes obvious that only the truth will set us free (John 8:32).

Paul loved Timothy enough to reprimand him. His motive was to help him, once again, get his priorities straight. Whether Timothy was by his own nature a timid person, as many are, the nature of God is one of boldness. That's why Paul wanted him to stir up the gift (the Holy Spirit) in him.

Let's see if we can give understanding, clarification, illumination as to what God has given to us His children. I believe with the comprehension or revelation of what we have received by God, our hearts should be pricked at our lack of Godlike faith.

Our constant blurts of frustration, periods of depression, lack of confidence in God, fear of persons or things is really a lack of trust or belief in God and His ability. It is really a deficiency of faith in the power of our God. Too many times we allow ourselves to be overwhelmed with the problems, the circumstances, the hardships of our life.

We have this uncanny ability to look at our problems which then turns them into some huge monster about to consume us. It's like Pilgrim or Christian's GIANT DESPAIR in Pilgrim's Progress.

We allow these things to overwhelm us, frighten us into a state of fear. Then we believe the situation will destroy or consume us (like the disciples in the boat). We are so beguiled with our self-made mountain that we take our eyes off Christ. Whereas, if we kept our eyes on Jesus, we would see that our mountains are merely mole hills or ant hills in comparison to God.

> Thus saith the Lord, the Heaven is my throne, and the earth is my footstool (Isaiah 66:1).

The earth is like a footstool to the vastness of God. Think of that. How small our problems are to the One who holds the whole world in His hand. Why do we allow ourselves to be so deceived by self? Why do we allow Satan to deceive us? Why do we yield our authority to the devil? Why do we stay so mindful of our problems?

It is because we do not truly or wholeheartedly trust God. We do not really know the power of God. Because of a lack of knowledge, we don't comprehend the power that God has endowed us with.

> My people are destroyed for a lack of knowledge (Hosea 4:6).

We are kept so busy with our problems, troubles, etc. that we neglect to study God's word. Therefore, we have a lack of knowledge. Consequently, the problems destroy us who have been given power or authority over Satan.

Because of a lack of knowledge, we are overwhelmed by things and are quitting. Many are running as cowards from the battle of life and are spiritually dying. I know that coward seems like a strong word. However, if we look closely at 2 Timothy 1:7 in our text, the word fear is translated more perfectly as cowardice.

That Scripture is saying that God has not given us a spirit of cowardice. This is fear that creates cowards like the soldier in battle who allows fear to grip him and he turns and runs away from the fight.

God has not nor ever will give us a spirit that runs from the fight. That spirit is not from God. He has given us of His Spirit. The Spirit of the Great I Am dwells within us. We can be sure that God is not or ever will be a coward and neither should we who are filled with His Spirit.

We quote Scripture, but how many times do we not understand it? Our life should be living and exhibiting Jesus. It is time to fully understand the words we speak and be strong in the Lord and in the power of His might (Ephesians 6:10).

Okay, let's get an understanding and knowing what God has not given us can help us to realize, to comprehend, to understand what God has given to us. First, our text tells us that God has given us the Spirit of power.

To help us realize the Spirit of power, let's make sure that we understand the meaning of the spirit of cowardice. Coward is defined as one who lacks courage in the face of danger, pain, or hardship.

God's soldiers don't have to run coward. We don't have to be afraid. God has given us the Spirit of power. It is imperative that we understand what that power is capable of doing if we are going to walk in Godlike faith.

Once we fully grasp hold of the fact that the spirit of cowardice or fear does not come from God, we are ready to comprehend what the Spirit of power means. We must understand that Satan wants the Church to be ignorant of Scripture. He knows that once God's soldiers have the revelation of what God has given through the Spirit of power, then we are victorious over his wiles and tactics. In other words, we have power over all his lies, his schemes, his plots, etc.

> Behold, I give unto you the power to tread on serpents and scorpions, and over ALL the power of the enemy: and nothing shall by any means hurt you (Luke 10:19).

Satan cannot overpower us unless we let him because we have yielded to the spirit of fear or cowardice instead of the Spirit of power. He will always get the better of any Christian in the flesh and not in the Spirit. However, when we yield to the Spirit of power or the Holy Spirit, we watch, stand fast in the faith, quit you like men, and be strong (1 Corinthians 16:13).

Quit you like men means that we fight like a man and not a coward. We don't run when the enemy comes. We are in watch for him and when he comes, we stand strong in the faith using the full armor of God as our weapons.

That again is how the one with the Spirit of power is recognized. We don't use carnal weapons to do warfare, but God's mighty weapons that pull-down Satan's strongholds (2 Corinthians 10:4). The devil is no match against us when we stand in the Spirit of power fully dressed in God's full armor.

God has also with the Spirit of power given us the Spirit of love. Our love for God and our devotion to Christ causes us to believe in His power and in His ability. If we are truly resting in the love of God and truly believing in His love for us, His perfect love casts out any fear trying to overtake us (1 John 4:18). The sad truth is that many of us fear and have torment because we don't really love God. However, when we love God with all our heart, with all our soul, with all our strength, and with all our mind, we have complete and total trust in God. That trust has no fear of any problem, trial, etc.

If we love God with all our being, His love is able to cast out the fears that try to torment us. God has not only given us the Spirit of love to love Him, but to love Jesus enough to speak boldly against whatever is contrary to Him and His word.

The Spirit of power gives us the boldness to be courageous and the Spirit of love makes us willing to do or to say whatever the Holy Spirit prompts us to do or say. That is what the Apostle Paul wanted Timothy to see and that is what the Holy Spirit wants us to see.

Now, the Spirit of a sound mind in the Greek means the Spirit of self-discipline or self-control. That signifies that we have the ability through the Holy Spirit to discipline ourselves according to the will of God.

> But I keep under my body, and bring it into subjection:
> lest that by any means, when I have preached to others,
> I myself should become a castaway (1 Corinthians 9:27).

We have the power of self-control. It is the power to keep our whole being in subjection to the Lord and to keep ourselves separated from the world and its evil powers. We have, because of God's love, the power to regulate our lives in accordance to the word of God which is the will of God.

When are God's soldiers going to stand for righteousness and speak LOUDLY against sin? When we love God, we will love our neighbor enough to tell them the truth no matter what. These are serious considerations. If we are of God, then we will not fear the consequences of standing for God and standing against all that is contrary to Him.

Furthermore, we will not be ashamed of those who are taking such a firm stand for God against the sin of this world and find ourselves persecuted by those in sin. Timothy had let himself forget the gift of the Holy Spirit in him and looked at Paul's persecution or imprisonment as a mountain of shame.

Perhaps, he was afraid that if he stood like Paul, he, too, would find himself in prison. Any of us can fall into such a temptation, but we must not remain there. Christ has given the authority over all Satan's spirits of fear, doubt, sickness, poverty, etc. through the power of the Holy Spirit. Paul was aware of what was going on with Timothy and reminded him to stir up the gift, to yield to the Holy Spirit in him, and to stand firm without wavering against whatever the devil was wielding his way.

Paul wanted Timothy to remember what Spirit that God had given to him. He needed to stir up that Spirit and be bold. God had not given him the spirit of cowardice that runs and hides from the battle.

As Jesus, Paul, etc. were enabled to stand against whatever the enemy sent their way through the power of the Holy Spirit, God has given us that Spirit that possesses Godlike faith. Through Him we have the power to overcome all storms, obstacles, strategies of Satan, etc. We have the love that enables us to love Him enough to stand against all the enemy's wiles and not run away as a coward. Then we have the Spirit of a sound mind which means that we have self-control to keep our body under subjection to His will. In short, Godlike faith is of the Holy Spirit and there is no fear or cowardice in Him!

Chapter 13

Godlike Faith Changes the Entailment

> In the eighth month, in the second year of Darius, came the word of the Lord unto Zechariah, the son of Berechiah, the son of Iddo the prophet, saying, The Lord hath been sore displeased with your fathers. Therefore say thou unto them, Thus saith the Lord of hosts; Turn ye unto me, saith the Lord of hosts, and I will turn unto you, saith the Lord of hosts. Be ye not as your fathers, unto whom the former prophets have cried, saying, Thus saith the Lord of hosts; Turn ye now from your evil ways, and from your evil doings: but they did not hear, nor hearken unto me, saith the Lord. Your fathers, where are they? and the prophets, do they live forever? But my words and my statutes, which I commanded my servants the prophets, did they not take hold of your fathers? and they returned and said, Like as the Lord of hosts thought to do unto us, according to our ways, and according to our doings, so hath he dealt with us (Zechariah 1:1-6).

To understand what this chapter is about, we will look at the word of the Lord to Zechariah. We are not going to look at his ten visions or that his prophecies concerning the Messiah are more particular than the other prophets.

God wants us to look at his message of repentance and deliverance with its subsequent blessings. In verse two, Zechariah announces that God was sore displeased with their fathers. They had heard with their ears, and their fathers told them of it, and their eyes have seen the woeful remains of it.

The broken-down temple was their evidence (physically) of God's displeasure with their fathers. What we need to understand about the judgments of God, which those that went before us were under, should be taken as warnings to us, so that we do not tread in their steps.

God is calling us to repentance, that we may cut off the entailment of the curse and get it turned into a blessing. What does that mean? It means that in order to cut off the entailment of the curse, we must repent.

Let me help us to understand what an entailment is. I'm sure most of us have read *Pride and Prejudice* by Jane Austen. The Bennet's estate was entailed upon Mr. Collins. According to an entailment, the estate or property could not be sold, but it must be inherited or bequeathed in a certain way.

Well, the sin of the father, the one who made the stipulation or entailment, was now the inheritance of the children. Now, let's understand that the entailment was a manmade law and could not be changed unless the law was changed.

It is similar to the law of sin with its curse passed down from generation to generation. Now, God is claiming in verse three that if we turn unto Him, He will turn unto us. That is saying that He will change the law or the entailment. In other words, repentance will change the entailed curses caused by the Fall.

> Be not deceived: God is not mocked: for whatsoever a man soweth, that shall he also reap. For he that soweth to his flesh shall of the flesh reap corruption: but he that soweth to the Spirit shall of the Spirit reap life everlasting (Galatians 6:7-8).

God is making clear in Galatians that He will not be mocked, He will not be scorned, and He will not be the subject of laughter or sport. We are not to deceive ourselves into thinking that God will not reward us according to our own sowing.

What we plant is what we receive. We can't plant a certain seed and expect to harvest something other than what we planted. God wants us to comprehend the entailment of curses on us and our children.

Let me give an example. Our father or mother could cop up an attitude at the drop of a hat. Well, as their progeny, their descendant, we have been willed or entailed by the law of sin and death and the law of sowing and reaping, the curse of copping up an attitude.

Okay, now, we, as part of our inheritance by law, also cop up an attitude at the drop of a hat. Likewise, it is quite noticeable in our children. Perhaps even to our displeasure. But our parents did not see that the law or entailment can be changed through repentance, so we inherited the bad or stinking attitude.

However, God, in His word, calls us to repentance or as Zechariah 1:3 says unto Himself. Listen up here. How can the entailment of the curses on our children be changed unless we change the law through the Great Lawgiver? How can we expect our children not to cop up a bad attitude, when we still do?

It is we that know that the entailment or law of inheritance, the law of sin and death, or the law of sowing and reaping can be changed. Why are we sowing a stinking attitude or any other sin in our life and in the life of our children, when we know that is what we are entailing to them? Yet, through repentance, we can change the entailment to ourselves and our children from curses to blessings.

To those of us who have read *Pride and Prejudice*, we know that it was asked how the Collin's could be happy with a property that was only entailed to them. Well, how can any of us, knowing the entailment of curses from the law of sin, not strive to change the entailment to the law of the Spirit with its entailment of life or blessings?

> And he shewed me Joshua the high priest standing before the angel of the Lord, and Satan standing at his right hand to resist him. And the lord said unto Satan, The Lord rebuke thee, O Satan; even the Lord that hath

GODLIKE FAITH CHANGES THE ENTAILMENT

chosen Jerusalem rebuke thee: is not this a brand plucked out of the fire? Now Joshua was clothed with filthy garments, and stood before the angel. And he answered and spake unto those that stood before him, saying, Take away the filthy garments from him. And unto him he said, Behold, I have caused thine iniquity to pass from thee, and I will clothe thee with change of raiment. And I said, Let them set a fair mitre upon his head. So they set a fair mitre upon his head, and clothed him with garments. And the angel of the Lord stood by. And the angel of the Lord protested unto Joshua, saying, Thus saith the Lord of hosts: If thou wilt walk in my ways, and if thou wilt keep my charge, then thou shalt also judge my house, and shalt also keep my courts, and I will give thee places to walk among these that stand by (Zechariah 3:1-7).

I could show these verses in a different manner, but for this book and this chapter, we will look at them as the law of entailment being changed from curses to blessings.

First of all, let me get back to Zechariah. He was sent on purpose by God to encourage the Jews to rebuild their temple and to restore the worship prescribed by Moses. In other words, they were to repent of receiving an entailment of the curses of the law of sin and death.

It left them without a temple, without the proper or correct mode of worship to God. They could not worship God in His prescribed way without the temple.

Now, repentance brings the means to start building the temple in which to properly worship God. This changes the curses to blessings. However, the devil who instigated the fathers to switch from blessings to curses is not at all pleased when we try to change the law of the entailment.

Zechariah 3:1 tells us that as Joshua, the high priest, stood before the Lord, Satan was standing at Joshua's right hand. Satan is the accuser, so he stands there before the Lord accusing Joshua of being a criminal. The devil is there as an advocate to the law. He is all for the entailment or the law of sin and death and its curses.

So, he constantly reminds the Lord and Joshua of the entailment that is passed down. It is the law and must be kept. However, praise the Lord. Let's look what the Lord says to Satan.

> And the Lord said unto Satan, the Lord rebuke thee, O Satan; even the Lord that hath chosen Jerusalem rebuke thee: is not this a brand plucked out of the fire (Zechariah 3:2).

God is about to reinstate the first law or the first entailment of blessings. We must understand that the curses were after man chose to switch from blessings to curses in the Garden of Eden.

Okay, God is changing the entailment because of repentance. As He is doing that, Satan comes before Him to accuse the repentant and to resist him. Listen here, the devil, when we come before the Lord opposes our service or worship. He tries to discourage us and claims that we are criminals who must keep the entailment of sin with its curses.

Yet, what does Zechariah see? God has Joshua, the high priest, rebuke Satan. He doesn't negotiate with him, but stops the devil's mouth immediately with a sharp reprimand or rebuke. The only way to deal with Satan is to say: "Get thee behind me, Satan." We must remember at all times, that we NOW have authority over him. Jesus gave it to us and shame on us if we don't walk in that authority or power over Satan.

Once the priest stands up to Satan, God changes the filthy garments, the entailment or the law of sin, death, and its curses to costly and righteous garments which are the entailment of the law of the Spirit.

Before we repent, we are imprisoned with the entailment of filthy garments of the curses of sin and death. We cannot change them even if we wanted to. They are our inheritance. Only if we change the law of the entailment can we have new garments of righteousness, life, and blessings.

Without repentance, we can rebuke Satan all we want, but our clothes or entailment are still filthy rags (Isaiah 64:6). However, once we are repentant, we can change our entailment. We can rebuke the devil of his entailment of the law of sin and death with its curses of sin, sickness, disease, debt, etc. that we had inherited.

It is time for us to comprehend that none of us have to keep ourselves imprisoned in the entailment of the old law of sin and death. We simply repent of our acceptance of the old entailment of the law of sin and its curses. Once we repent, we are no longer prisoner to sin and its consequences. In other words, we are set free from all that happened at the Fall. Christ has given us power or authority over all Satan's power. The only thing that we don't have power over in this life is the time of our death. Unless, God has said it is time for us to depart and be with Him, we take the authority over sin, sickness, disease, debt, etc. in the Name of Jesus.

Once we understand our authority, we stand in that power. Our old filthy garments will be changed from the old entailment of sin, death, and its curses to the new garments in Christ of the law of the Spirit of life and His blessings!

Chapter 14

Godlike Faith Walks In Authority Over Satan

Then certain of the vagabond Jews, exorcists, took upon them to call over them which had evils spirits the name of the Lord Jesus, saying, We adjure you by Jesus whom Paul preacheth. And there were seven sons of one Sceva, a Jew, and chief of the priests, which did so. And the evil spirit answered, and said, Jesus I know, and Paul I know; but who are ye? And the man in whom the evil spirit was leaped on them, and overcame them, and prevailed against them, so that they fled out of that house naked and wounded (Acts 19:13-16).

THIS chapter is not so much concerned with our text as it is in the principle that the Lord wants us to comprehend. These verses in Acts help illuminate Godlike faith and man's faith.

Many of God's soldiers are receiving similar reactions as those of the sons of Sceva. It is not because we are not Christ's as these were not. It is because we are ignorant or unaware of our enemy. We tend to walk in our own understanding or what we think is best for our life with little or no comprehension of God's word. Without knowing what Christ has given to God's soldiers, we will not walk in Godlike faith.

> Lest Satan should get an advantage of us: for we ae not ignorant of his devices (2 Corinthians 2:11).

This Scripture has a two-fold meaning that is imperative that we grasp.

1. The first meaning is that because we are not ignorant of Satan's devices, Satan won't get the advantage over us.
2. The second meaning is that if we are ignorant of Satan's devices, he will get the advantage over of us.

When the devil gets the advantage over a Christian, he or she (the Christian) comes out of the encounter like the sons of Sceva. We flee like cowards or the conquered. Our flesh takes control and we become disheartened, discouraged, and spiritually weakened.

The sad part is that when this happens or when trouble or calamity hit, we blame God. But the blame is really ours. It is not God's fault when we claim to be His child and are ignorant of Satan's devices, his cunning, his trickery, or his methods.

> My people are destroyed for lack of knowledge: because thou hast rejected knowledge, I will also reject thee (Hosea 4:6).

Hosea reveals the law of reciprocity. In other words, it is the results of what happens when something is done. Let me give an example of reciprocity. We work and the employer pays us. So, when God says if we do something that He will do this or that, it means that He reciprocates or returns. According to Hosea, God is saying that because we have rejected His knowledge, His laws, or His principles, He will reject the rejectors.

> Study to shew thyself approved unto God, a workman that needeth not to be ashamed, rightly dividing the word of truth (2 Timothy 2:15).

For any of us today, that claim to be a Christian, to lack knowledge or to be ignorant of Satan's devices is intentional. That may seem harsh, but it is truth. We have access to much media of the word of God. There is not only the written word, but it is available on CD's, etc.

There is no excuse for us to be ignorant. If we are, we have intentionally chosen to reject the knowledge that would keep us from being destroyed.

I don't know how many times that I have heard Christians claim that there isn't time to read the Bible because of their work schedule, etc. Yet, they have time to play games, watch television, go out to eat, or whatever. Because of this, Satan and his demons are getting the advantage of us. Christians, who are not to be ignorant of Satan's devices, seem to be as ignorant of the things of God and the tactics of Satan as were the sons of Sceva.

> Let this mind be in you which was also in Christ Jesus (Philippians 2:5).

Think of that. Was Jesus ignorant of Satan's devices, cunning, methods, or stratagems? Of course not. He knew the modus operandi of Satan. Jesus knew how the enemy works. Because He knew His enemy, He knew how to combat or to overcome all the tactics or motives of the forces of evil.

As Christ recognized and knew the enemy, Satan and the demons knew Christ. Let's understand something here. Satan and his demons, the fallen angels who follow him, are personal intelligences.

The devil is a real spirit personality and so are his demons. What does the word personality mean. The simplest definition is the power of thinking, the power of feeling, and the power of willing. It's time for us to realize that Satan has intelligence that is keener, sharper, and smarter than our intelligence. That means that the intelligence of Satan and his demons who are also spirit personalities is more acute than the intellect that we possess.

No matter how smart or how intellectual we may be, we will never outsmart or out maneuver the forces of Satan in the natural. Yet, the Church insists upon being led by carnal or worldly ways. We use our own understanding or whatever else is from the flesh or sensual. Then when forced to face Satan, we find ourselves running away like the sons of Sceva.

Listen to me, if we are to be wiser than Satan and his hosts, it must be through the Spirit. As the devil is a spirit personality, so is God, the Holy Spirit. But this Spirit is the Creator of the other spirits.

That's why it is essential that we become true worshippers that worship the Father in Spirit and in truth (John 4:24). We have to apprehend that the devil is not only smarter (has far superior intelligence over us), but he is spirit. We are flesh and blood and we cannot battle with spirit beings.

> For though we walk in the flesh, we do not war after the flesh: For the weapons of our warfare are not carnal, but mighty through God to the pulling down of strong holds (2 Corinthians 10:3-4).

Yes, we live or walk in the natural or fleshly because we are flesh and blood. But we cannot war after the natural. As many Christians have found out. The weapons that we are to use must be God's. Why is that so? Because ONLY God is wiser and more intelligent than Satan and the demons.

Only God is Omniscient or all knowing; He is the Creator of knowledge. If Satan and his diabolical crew can get us in the flesh, we are beaten before we start. That is like an ant thinking it can battle us. Quite a joke. However, that is exactly what we look like to Satan and the demons in our flesh. Simply put, we are crushed before we start.

> The thief cometh not, but for to steal, and to kill, and to destroy: I am come that they might have life, and that they might have it more abundantly (John 10:10).

Satan comes to bring death (spiritual death). Christ comes to bring life (spiritual life). Think of that. Now, let's look at the Christians that we know. Are they more spiritual than carnal? Do they spend most of their time in carnality, the cares and things of this world?

Do they complain, bicker, call people names, etc.? Do they discuss spiritual things or things of little value when compared to the spiritual things of God? If they are more carnal than spiritual, they are imprisoned by Satan who is keeping them carnally influenced. He is setting them up to destroy them. They are heading for spiritual shipwreck.

God's soldiers must be transformed from the likeness of this world into the likeness of Christ. This is only accomplished by the renewing, the renovating, the refurbishing, the repairing of our minds (Romans 12:2). As long as we continue to partake of this world and its way, our mind will never be renewed. The only way for our mind to be transformed from fleshly minded to spiritually minded is changing the media it is programmed with.

Too many Christians are not reading, studying, and meditating upon the word of God, which is the only way to receive the mind of Christ. This means the thinking, the discerning, the reasoning, etc. of Christ. When we walk in the mind of Christ, we no longer walk in our natural mind and its carnality.

> Be sober, be vigilant; because your adversary the devil, as a roaring lion, walketh about, seeking whom he may devour: whom resist steadfast in the faith (1 Peter 5:8-9a).

This is a hard truth, but many in the Church are not sober. We are intoxicated with the things of the flesh and the love of the world. We are not vigilant. Many of us are so ignorant of Satan's desire and tactics for our destruction, that we march right alongside of him. By the time, many of us realize who we are yielding to, it is too late. For we have been destroyed or devoured as the sons of Sceva.

Satan and his demons never slithered upon Jesus, Paul, etc. They were watching for him. Their heart was tuned into God, their eyes were anointed with spiritual eye salve, and they could hear and see what God saw.

God knows every move the devil is making, and He knows the moves he will make before he makes them. That is why those with the mind of Christ who walk in Spirit and in truth are not taken off guard by the enemy. Don't get me wrong, the devil will still come as he did with Christ. However he doesn't have to win over us.

> Behold I give unto you power to tread on serpents and scorpions, and over all the power of the enemy: and nothing shall by any means hurt you (Luke 10:19).

Okay, why are the serpents and scorpions stealing, killing, and destroying in the lives of so many of us professing to belong to Christ? It's quite simple. Just because we have the authority doesn't mean that we walk in it.

This authority or power is not a carnal, fleshly, or natural authority, it is a spiritual or supernatural authority. It is letting Christ's mind think in us. In fact, it is being crucified with Christ and living by His faith or Godlike faith (Galatians 2:20).

It is us standing in the natural realm that we see, but it is having no fleshly part in the standing. We yield ourselves to Christ, and then our spirit being is one with His. It is then Jesus standing in the spirit world. In other words, the devil sees us, but he also sees Him Who is in us.

As we submit ourselves to God, resist Satan, he will flee from us (James 4:7). Listen to me, Satan is no match for Jesus Christ Who is his Creator. He is well aware that Jesus will destroy him in the end (Matthew 8:29). It is us who must grasp the truth that Satan has no power or authority over us who walk in Spirit and in truth.

Yet, how many of us constantly walk in the flesh or carnality? God wants us to get out of ourselves, our selfish pleasures, and stand against the devil as His soldiers fully armed in His full armor. He has done all to give us the authority over Satan. Now, He expects us to take that authority, walk in it, and be victorious.

We must quit trying to fight a spirit with supernatural powers with our natural or fleshly weapons. Satan knows that if he can keep us in the flesh, he can keep us defeated. God's soldiers must stop playing tiddly winks with the devil and letting him win.

Let's be honest, we should know the difference between our being in the flesh and in the Spirit. We need to stop yielding to our flesh and start yielding to God. Time to put our flesh and its lust under and bring our body into subjection to Christ. We must stop being the victim when we are the victor.

It is time for God's soldiers to remember that it was through His faith that He created all things. God's faith is capable of doing the impossible. When we became born again and filled with the Holy Spirit of God, He gave us all a measure of faith that is capable of doing the impossible through Him. We are not the ones doing the impossible, but God through us. Godlike faith rises in us and enables God to be God and do what is impossible to man.

This book's intention was to illuminate Godlike faith in God's soldiers. It is essential that we know that we know that we have authority over Satan and that he has no authority over us. As we walk in the mind of Christ, we have Godlike faith that gives no place to the devil, his demons, or his diabolical plans to destroy us. We are aware of Satan, his designs, his tactics, his obstacles, etc., and they are prohibited from prospering. God's soldiers yield to the mind of Christ, walk in Godlike faith, stand in God's full armor, and give no opportunity for Satan to take authority over us!

www.ingramcontent.com/pod-product-compliance
Lightning Source LLC
Chambersburg PA
CBHW071159090426
42736CB00012B/2386